THE BIRTH OF THE
RT

Tony Beard

Capital Transport

Introduction

On 12 February 1954, A A M Durrant, Chief Mechanical Engineer (Road Services) for London Transport, penned a memorandum to his Executive regarding the disposal of RT 19. In noting that the vehicle had not been used for some time, he sought authority to hand over the chassis to the Chiswick Training School for demonstration work in the classroom. Agreeing to this action, the Executive also consented to Durrant's second request that the body from RT 19, which had been described as being in poor condition, should be destroyed following the recovery of usable parts. It appears somewhat ironic that the bus body that Durrant was sentencing to death had been built for RT 1 in 1939; he had masterminded its inception.

The formative years proved difficult for the prototype RT and the production batch of 150 vehicles that followed, their planning and construction taking place against a background of deepening crisis in Europe.

Fortunately, there survives in the safekeeping of TfL's Group Archives and Records Custody Service a significant collection of documents that refer to the development of the RT. Much of the information they contain has not previously appeared in print. My heartfelt thanks goes to Philip Wood and Emma Theophilus Wright, who have now departed for pastures new, and to Beth Mercer and members of her team, past and present, for coping with my many demands on their service by listing and sourcing many files. Further research was undertaken at London Transport Museum's Depot at Acton where Antony Roskoss, John Marshall and Les Hampton provided many important items. AEC material is mainly held in three locations: the British Commercial Vehicle Museum at Leyland, Warwick University and the Heritage Motor Centre at Gaydon and visits to each were most rewarding. Finally, my thanks to my wife Lynne, who has been of great support, and Jim Whiting for having faith in the fact that this book would eventually be written.

Tony Beard

First published 2011

ISBN 978 185414 351 8

Published by Capital Transport Publishing
www.capitaltransport.com

Printed by 1010 Printing International Ltd

Photo credits
G H F Atkins 43
S J Butler 84
Alan B Cross 18, 22 centre and bottom, 83 bottom, 88 top
W H R Godwin 91, 95 bottom
W J Haynes 41, 42 60
Imperial War Museum 35, 37, 44 left
Dave Jones/LCCTT 29
C F Klapper 24, 25, 43
London Transport Museum 8, 11, 12, 22 top, 44 right, 46, 50, 52, 58, 63, 64, 67, 75, 76, 77, 79, 92, 93, 95 top
S A Newman 82
TfL Archives 10, 57, 70
Weymann 81

The paintings on the cover and on page 13 are by Barry Pearce

Contents

A New Bus

On 5th August 1937, A A M Durrant, then holding the appointment of Chief Engineer (Buses and Coaches) for the London Passenger Transport Board, presented a memorandum to its Engineering Committee in which he reviewed the progress of designs for double deck buses constructed for service in the capital. In his landmark submission, Durrant sought approval for the Board to build, in conjunction with the Associated Equipment Company, an experimental double deck bus as a prototype that would allow production to commence in 1939.

Durrant's career had begun in October 1919 when he entered into the employment of the London General Omnibus Company as a technical assistant. By 1931, he had achieved the position of Assistant Chief Engineer, assuming the appointment of Chief Engineer in 1935. In promoting a partnership between the Board and AEC to build the new bus, Durrant was calling on years of previous collaboration that had seen a series of vehicles produced for service in the capital, the design of which exploited the expertise of his team of engineers at the Board's Chiswick works and those of G J Rackham at the Southall works of AEC.

The AEC Regent chassis, soon to be identified with the project, had been introduced in 1928, its popularity enhanced by its purchase in significant quantities by the LGOC and later the LPTB. In 1933, AEC had become the Board's preferred supplier of chassis under the continuance of an agreement dating back to the company's formation in 1912 brought about by the separation from the LGOC of its considerable bus building and repair works at Walthamstow. The deal was brokered by the Chairman of the Underground Group, Albert Stanley, later Lord Ashfield.

In a report produced in May 1937, Durrant injected a note of concern regarding the supply of materials for new rolling stock, which had caused modification to an earlier proposal for the introduction of metal bodywork at Chiswick. Previous plans had proposed to introduce an all-metal form of construction for the 10T10 single deck bodies due to be built in the early part of 1938. But having regard for the difficulty in obtaining steel, these proposals had been abandoned and an improved form of composite (metal/timber) construction was introduced.

On 4 November 1937, the biennial Commercial Motor Show transferred from its previous location at Olympia to the newly opened Earls Court Exhibition Centre where it became the last held before the declaration of war with Germany. No doubt in order to gain first hand knowledge of the latest developments in the bus building industry, the Board despatched a member of its staff to the show. The account he subsequently submitted described the AEC stand as the most popular, closely followed by that of Leyland with oil engines powering a large proportion of the vehicles on display. Attracting much attention on the AEC stand was Leeds City Transport double deck bus 400, where it was exhibited carrying the name Leeds City Pullman. The locally built Roe body was the brainchild of the operator's Chief Engineer, Vane Moreland, representing a departure in design by the continuance of the rounded appearance introduced by the manufacturer but now employing a four-bay layout between the front and rear bulkheads with noticeably deeper windows. Passenger safety was exemplified on this vehicle by an emergency brake having been fitted in the form of a rope pull on the rear platform and attached to the lower deck front bulkhead.

It is interesting to note the areas that the LPTB reporter considered worthy of mention. Under the heading 'bodies' his first comparison summarised the types of opening windows installed. Of the ten vehicles inspected most were built with half drop lights from a variety of manufacturers or plain sliding fanlights, and nearly all were additionally fitted with louvred windows. Some of the interior lighting systems were considered too fancy, many lights being positioned where they might be struck by passengers. He also discovered that Rexine or leather seating was more plentiful than the moquette favoured by the Board.

Another area of evaluation centred upon the type of floor slatting adopted, the most popular being plain oak with steel strips on the stairways only. A bus from the West Yorkshire company used rubber floor strips, oak platform slats and alloy stair treads. Rubber fringes to the platforms, as installed on STL types, appeared popular but in general, such edging was metal.

Traffic indicators were scarce, only two vehicles being so equipped. Several buses did not have a recessed driver's step; on these, access to the cab was gained by using an aluminium step ring on the wheel hub. Where fitted to the vehicles on display, bumpers consisted of a single bar close to the rear panel or miniature bumpers fitted to the offside rear corner. Two vehicles had wings made from a rubber composition. Surprisingly, one item considered in detail was the provision of used ticket boxes, 14 vehicles receiving careful scrutiny. Of these, 12 were found to replicate the box used by the Board, one had no used ticket facility and the last example had a box by the staircase.

The Leyland stand did have a vehicle built for London Transport on display: an F1 class trolleybus (753). However, no space was found here for the TF single deck coach, the prototype of which had made its debut in July, although an article on its construction appeared in the show edition of *Commercial Motor*. Built following two years of collaboration between Leyland Motors and the Board, the TF was equipped with a rotary compressor driven from the engine that supplied air for braking and for operation of the pre-select mechanism for changing gear.

In conclusion, the Board's reporter considered the most practical and well-designed chassis at the show was the AEC Regal II, an example of which was displayed on the company's stand. He returned from Earl's Court with the major manufacturers' catalogues, some of which contained a price list; for comparison, an AEC Regent chassis fitted with an oil engine was £1,425 while a similarly equipped Leyland TD5 was £1,210.

Writing in the autumn of 1937 for the *Commercial Motor*, LPTB chairman Lord Ashfield laid great emphasis on a widely held conviction that passenger vehicles must be as attractive to the public as the car. In support, he recorded that by September 1936, the number of private cars on the road was approximately 1,643,000, this figure representing an increase of 170,000 over the 1935 figure. Although the number for 1937 remained unpublished at the time, it was known to have been approaching the 1,825,000 mark. Ashfield therefore charged each engineer and designer to seek perfection, an ideal, which he knew, had yet to be reached. And in conclusion Ashfield listed for development: further improvement of the compression injection engine, the elimination of noise, the elimination of the human factor in gear changing, the improvement of vehicle suspension with a view to enhancing riding qualities, better ventilation and the perfection of lighting and seating.

AEC was anxious about its reputation and, in mid-November 1937, the Company's Home Sales Manager, A S C Chattey gave directors his opinion of the current situation which he had formed having reviewed the company's sales prospects during the recent Commercial Motor Show. In his report, Chattey reflected upon the qualities in performance demonstrated by the engines of Gardner and Leyland manufacture. In addition, once established in any given undertaking, the dominance by chassis of the Daimler company (using Gardner engines) and the Leyland company using its own engines was such that it was almost impossible for AEC to gain a foothold.

Chattey also stated that in his view, current models in the AEC range had no superiority over the Daimler/Gardner or Leyland products to justify a prospective purchaser paying a higher price for the AEC. This situation was by no means improved by the failure in service of recent versions of the AEC oil engine that had caused a lack of confidence in the company's output by important passenger vehicle operators. In agreeing that there was indeed cause for dissatisfaction, AEC's directors felt that remedial steps should immediately be taken by the introduction of a programme of more intensive research in order that an oil engine could be produced at least equal, if not superior, to those produced by the company's principal competitors.

On 14 October 1937, an agreement was signed supplemental to one between the LPTB and the Associated Equipment Company of 6 December 1933, the most significant effect of which was to vary the number of bus and coach chassis and their associated spare parts that AEC was required to supply and sell to the Board, and which the Board was required to purchase. The new agreement had in fact already come into effect from 1 July 1937 and, as a yearly quota was now prescribed, the expiry date of the original agreement was extended from 5 December 1943 to 30 June 1944. Under this AEC had been required to supply chassis and spare parts for 4,500 buses. According to the first draft of the supplemental agreement, AEC would now supply 75% of the Board's bus and coach chassis and spare parts (excluding vehicles with a seating capacity not exceeding 20 passengers). By the time the first draft appeared, the figure of 75% had been raised to 80%. Calculations revealed that AEC could now supply an additional 400 vehicles over the seven-year period while the agreement was in force.

Meanwhile, London Transport had decided to conduct a test that compared the performance of the Leyland STD against that of the AEC STL. The report, issued in May 1938, gave a brief synopsis of the STD, 100 of which had been placed in service the previous year. Although the chassis was a standard Leyland product, it contained modifications considered essential to meet the Board's operating requirements such as AEC worm and nut steering. The body, modelled on the standard Chiswick product, was built by Leyland but using a metal frame, the company borrowing the body from STL 1217 for the purpose. The specification applied to the STD included several features that did not conform to the standard required of the AEC STL. For example, 90 of the vehicles were fitted with crash gearboxes and the remaining 10 with Lysholm-Smith torque converters, fuel consumption of the vehicles so fitted increasing by 0.7mpg when compared with the AEC fluid transmission. The gearboxes were found to be extremely noisy in operation, especially following a period of service, and inferior to the pre-select gearbox operation that was now standard on AEC chassis produced for the Board. The absence of a quieter transmission deemed as unlikely the purchase of additional double deck vehicles in great quantity from Leyland unless the Board adjusted its specification for further buses from the supplier. However, the performance of the STDs was found extremely satisfactory, even surpassing that obtained from the AEC vehicles, particularly in relation to the engine and brakes.

In June 1939, the Board requested a second report comparing the STD with the STL and, for evaluation purposes, STLs at Battersea garage were selected as being of similar age to the Leylands. Running statistics were taken for a period of 13 weeks from September to December 1938, thus allowing 12 months to elapse between reports. The data collected found that although there had been an improvement in the AEC product, the STD remained the better vehicle.

When writing of AEC's pre-war achievements, most authorities agree that the first major development in bigger engine design came with the specification applied to the 10T10 single deck coaches of 1938 that called for an 8.8 litre unit. Designated A180, the six-cylinder, direct injection, compression ignition engine was of new construction and so not interchangeable with those fitted to past variants of the T series. Nevertheless, there were some misgivings relating to the performance of the new engine. In a document produced by the Board's Rolling Stock and Operating Departments Committee regarding the type, the initial criticism refers to the poor acceleration in first and second gears, supported with the comment that "an STL when loaded leaves a 10T10 standing". This prompted adjustments to the fuel pump settings.

Under experiment S5006, the engine noise of the A180 was compared with the Leyland 8.6 litre engine fitted to the STD. The subsequent report concluded that although both units were practically identical, the Leyland unit was considerably quieter. Arrangements were therefore made for a 10T10 to be fitted with a Leyland engine so that the results from the Leyland unit might be matched with the A180 when used in an identical chassis/body combination, thus eliminating the differences in STD body construction. The installation called for some special adaptations such as the manufacture of special dumb irons and the fitting of a fluid flywheel to the Leyland engine. The comparison showed that, immediately after fitting, the Leyland engine was still the quieter and, once the AEC engine had undergone some modification, road tests were carried out. The Leyland engine did become noticeably noisier after completing some 70,300 miles; the AEC unit seized after 42,000 although its mpg had been better. The question of materials used in the AEC engine became the subject of a dialogue between the Board and AEC and some improvements were made which influenced the design of later units.

Pre-dating AEC's recognition that the quality of its oil engines must improve came a number of exchanges with London Transport regarding the A180. On 5 November 1937, Durrant sent a letter to R McDonald, the Board's Solicitor, outlining correspondence that had taken place with Leyland and AEC regarding the AEC engine and seeking confirmation that all necessary action had been taken to safeguard the Board's interest. Of concern to the Chief Engineer was the patent relating to the A180, Durrant recording that until production commenced, AEC had no direct injection engine that was satisfactory for use in London. Moreover, when the engine in the Leyland STDs was seen as an improvement over the standard AEC product, AEC had been compelled to produce the A180.

Upon examination, it soon became apparent that the design of the direct injection A180 was similar to that of Leyland's engine; furthermore, in order for the Board to obtain optimum performance from the engine, it became necessary to fit fuel injection nozzles that were identical to those of Leyland manufacture. It was due to this situation that the Board's Technical Officer requested AEC to furnish him with some evidence regarding the company's non-infringement of the Leyland patent, which was subsequently sent to the Board in the shape of a Patent Agent's report. Later, however, AEC indicated that it might ask the Board, by its use of the engine, to indemnify the company against patent action, which, according to Durrant, revealed the company's nervousness about the whole situation. E C Ottaway, the Board's Technical Officer had replied to the effect that, as the Board had specified an engine that AEC had subsequently designed, he would expect the company to indemnify the Board. Concurrently a letter to Leyland Motors brought a response that Leyland had no objection to its design of nozzle being employed provided that it was not used in conjunction with any patents they held.

Presumably, McDonald considered the points raised by Durrant required a response from his senior officer, A H Grainger, the Board's Solicitor (General). Grainger immediately examined all correspondence available on the subject and concluded that the Board did not want to be disadvantaged by its agreement with AEC in the knowledge that Leyland Motors had produced an engine that was more satisfactory. He noted that a request was made by the Board for AEC to produce an engine comparable to the Leyland product and upon its completion, an order was placed specifying the chassis in which it was to be used. Had the agreement with AEC not existed the Board could have approached another manufacturer specifying the type of engine required. However, AEC would still be required to cover the Board against any liability should it be later found that its engine infringed the Leyland patent.

AEC responded that it was satisfied that no patent had been infringed although it was not prepared to indemnify the Board. However, Durrant no doubt wished to bring about a swift conclusion to the situation mindful that, just two months earlier, he had instigated development in collaboration with AEC of the 1939 double deck bus. To pursue the issue further, Ottaway became involved; replies coming from R F Fryars, AEC's Secretary and Treasurer. A breakthrough occurred on 1 February 1938 when Fryars wrote to Grainger outlining details of a consultation he had had the previous day with Sir Stafford Cripps and a Mr Mould, both learned in the law of patents, the latter specifically in the matter of Patent Specifications. Seizing on the opportunity, Fryars had taken up the issue of any infringement of the Leyland patent by AEC. Both learned gentlemen were positive in their assessment that no infringement existed and that there were no grounds for concern that AEC might be attacked on such allegation. Fryars concluded by requesting that the Board abandon its request for an indemnity from AEC, which following one last exchange appears to have been the case. Contemporary accounts indicate that the A180 engine was manufactured by AEC under licence from Leyland but the foregoing provides us with an alternative view.

When drawing up the specification for a new bus, the Board's engineers were not only required to consider regulations that governed construction but also to be mindful of continuous development, one such area relating to transmission, the design of which was required to overcome a fundamental weakness of the engine caused by the absence of torque (turning effort) at very low speeds. To overcome this weakness, it was necessary to provide a slipping device or clutch to enable a bus to be driven from rest with the engine rotating at minimum speed. By the mid-1930s, a heavy strain was being imposed on the transmission fitted to the Board's buses due to the number of stops and starts per mile and the constant braking and acceleration. The specification applied to the clutch and gearbox required a vehicle to be started from rest without shudder and changes of gear accomplished with a minimum of manual effort by the driver.

The Board recognised that driving a bus in the capital produced driver fatigue and that his exertions should be reduced as much as possible. In consequence, a decision was taken to replace the orthodox clutch and crash gearbox with a fluid transmission comprising a Wilson pre-selective epicyclic gearbox and fluid flywheel. This innovation replaced the clutch whose characteristic slip was automatically made available through hydraulic means; consequently, the clutch pedal became the gear-change pedal. Also of great benefit was the design of the gearbox, which eliminated the extreme accuracy required to judge engine speed when changing gear.

Unfortunately, the Board soon became aware that, in spite of the greater ease and simplicity offered by a fluid transmission, the system led to many cases of incorrect handling and, in a number of instances, undeniable abuse. Upward changes of gear were made with a fully activated accelerator, showing deliberate disregard for the operating regulations that required its total release. Additionally the gear change pedal was brought into use when vehicles pulled away from rest, infringing yet another instruction. Attempts were made to curtail such practices by the introduction of a torque converter, a hydraulic device that replaced both clutch and gearbox, but its efficiency was relatively low and, as previously recorded, resulted in a subsequent increase in fuel consumption. However, development continued and the torque converter became considered a serious competitor for introduction in the Central Area.

STL 857 (later STF1) entered service in November 1935, its streamlined styling being partly perpetuated on the RT, most noticeably in the forward profile of the body. In failing to continue a beading line above the upper front deck windows, it became necessary to bring the silver roof colour to a point just above the front destination panel. The entrance to the cab no doubt influenced the design of that initially chosen for RT 1. Later, the viability of full fronted cabs became the subject of dispute between Eric Ottaway and S R Geary, whose opinions were sought in their capacities as senior Board officers when the design of the post-war fleet was under consideration.

In 1939, Ottaway reported on the merits of the three major types of transmission that had been used by the Board. He also mentioned the testing of a fully automatic gearbox produced by A A Miller but despite some relative success following some 18,000 miles under normal conditions, he concluded that there was no place on London streets for a bus with fully automatic gears.

The braking systems installed on oil engined road vehicles had also caused difficulties for the design teams. On petrol-engined vehicles, vacuum braking assistance was provided which became available upon the driver closing the throttle. However, oil engines required a full charge of air irrespective of the amount of fuel injected and it became necessary to provide a vacuum pump (or exhauster) driven from the engine. Nevertheless, this device could swiftly drain the vacuum tank and in consequence, a great deal of research had been undertaken to cover instances when the footbrake was frequently used at low speed in congested traffic. Despite an application of the handbrake being amply sufficient to stop a bus in such circumstances, the prevailing regulations did not permit this solution to the problem.

But the main difficulty associated with braking was the continuous variation in adjustment as normal wear proceeded. A device known as the RP automatic brake adjuster, named after its designers Messrs Rowlands (Chief Engineer) and Parker (his assistant) of the City of Birmingham Transport Department, had been introduced on the latest vehicles to reduce frequent brake lining adjustment and preserve a more consistent standard of braking; it was spectacularly successful. Although original development work had been carried out by Daimler, the patent rights were eventually sold to Clayton Dewandre Limited, which became responsible for the design and supply of RP brake adjuster material to interested manufacturers and operators. Daimler continued to manufacture the adjusters for its own vehicles.

There also existed a necessity for an effective form of springing due to the uneven road surfaces over which buses were driven; the theory used here being that ease of riding was proportional to the permitted deflection of the suspension system. On buses, effective suspension was brought about by means of two factors: the road springs and tyres, with passengers enjoying a third through the seat cushions. However, increased deflection of springs caused excessive roll upon cornering and devices known as stabilisers became necessary which, while allowing the normal function of road springs, prevented any excessive lateral movement.

Body construction was limited by regulations governing width and length with height being established by consideration of wheelarches, headroom and restrictions imposed by garage clearance features. Another consideration was the placing of external advertisements which were in direct competition with the position of the route indicator for the space available. Special attention had been given to the design of the route indicators in order that they could provide the maximum amount of information in the most legible manner. As vehicles were required to show all variations of routes operated by the garage to which they were allocated, this sometimes resulted in 39ft-long blinds being fitted. However, not appreciated by many was that by installing blind boxes and their associated mechanisms and illumination, an unavoidable weakening of the body structure resulted whose subsequent strengthening added to the overall weight.

A recently introduced practice was the blending of the floor to the side lining panels in order to eliminate dirt-collecting areas; the absence of ledges around windows served similar purpose. Experience had shown that in the Central Area, the rear entrance vehicle was favoured in order to deal with the rapid loading and unloading of passengers. The maximum possible amount of space was therefore allocated to the rear platform necessitating a degree of ingenuity when planning layout of the lower deck seating.

Planning to Prototype

Convening at Southall on 4 October 1937, with C W Reeve in the chair, AEC directors received a report from their Chief Engineer, G J Rackham, regarding a special design of the new vehicle for the London Passenger Transport Board, in which he recorded departures in almost every essential respect from the specification to which London Transport vehicles were then being built. He listed the principal new characteristics as rubber mounting of the engine, an automatically adjustable compressed air braking system, pneumatic control of speed changing mechanism, centre point steering, operation of power driven accessories from the gearbox, centrifugally operated automatic clutch, improved springing, modified epicyclic gearbox and low-pressure tyres.

The draft design details for the chassis had been in the possession of AEC for approximately one month having been previously presented on 1 September 1937 to the Joint Experimental Committee. This Committee comprised representatives from the LPTB and AEC, its meetings being held at AEC's Southall Works on a fortnightly basis. The JEC's main function was to consider continuing development and improvements to the Board's motor bus fleet and, if necessary, an experiment would be allocated to particular components or complete projects with subsequent testing overseen by Chiswick or Southall. By the time of the next JEC meeting on 15 September, the project had received the designation '1939 Double Deck Vehicle'.

Late November saw experiment S4810 allocated to the new chassis, together with the initial classification, 16STL. Discussion now centred upon its power source: an 8.8 litre engine that would be completed by 1 March 1938 and fitted with a pot combustion chamber if this refinement attracted positive comment from the Board's Engineers. A short postponement was requested in order to consider the final design and experiment S4754 was issued to cover subsequent testing. Alternatively, toroidal heads and pistons could have been installed, amid claims that engines so equipped gave improved performance. A statement issued in support commented that 'the employment of a toroidal engine would be an advantage, if future policy called for faster engine acceleration characteristics, since this unit has a greater reserve of power than the pot engine because a greater quantity of fuel may be injected per stroke into the toroidal engine without causing dirty exhaust'. The decision regarding the design of the engine was now placed firmly with the LPTB whose engineers subsequently decided that three examples should be supplied with toroidal heads and installed in STLs 2513-2515, an additional unit with a pot type combustion chamber being produced for the prototype chassis and classified A182. Later, one of the three STLs had its 'special engine' replaced by a standard A173 used to power later variants of the type; the unit removed was retained to provide parts for the two remaining examples.

On 24 November 1937, the drawing office at Chiswick issued a general arrangement plan for the new bus. Although the shape of earlier models could be seen in the drawing, the styling of the body owed much to the streamline era, which continued to have a profound effect on the designers of the world's road, rail, air and seaborne transport. According to some writers, the passion for such accentuation excelled female fashion in exaggeration. The Board's view was that streamlining should be applied to an object where it did not impede movement; bus bodies were therefore built without any sharp corners to portray a flowing shape. A similar functional style was required of the interior,

Opposite: The first plans for the body were completed on 24 November 1937 and despite many obvious changes that would later occur, the overall RT shape is easily recognised although when the drawing was produced, the bus was known only as the 1939 Double Deck Vehicle. Most noticeable is the absence of a cab door, this area replicating to some degree the style of STF 1, the upper angle of the small window to the rear of the cab predicting the unique angled shape applied to the top of the door designed for the prototype.

Below: The extension from the front bulkhead to provide a fixing for a rubber front wing was individually tested on two STL vehicles with some degree of success, as the design was included in the body specifications for the 10T10 and RT. Also of note is the similarity of the bonnet area of the 10T10 and the body for RT 1 as originally drawn although its bonnet plate was placed further forward.

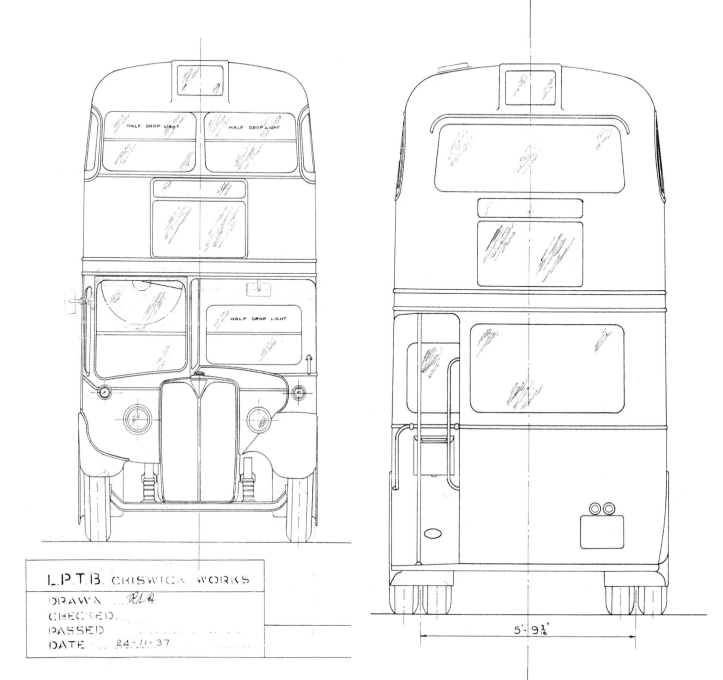

HALF DROP LIGHT   HALF DROP LIGHT

HALF DROP LIGHT

5'-9½"

in order to provide a bright and restful ambience underlined by the absence of unnecessary decoration. Drawn within days following the closure of the 1937 Commercial Motor Show, the influence of the four bay body built for Leeds Corporation was obvious, although the Board's draughtsmen had not been swayed by the deeper windows that featured in the Roe example. Many differences exist between the first plan and the body as finally produced; however, most obvious in offside elevation is the absence of a cab door, the area assuming a shape similar to that applied to STF 1. This vehicle (originally numbered STL 857) had entered service in November 1936; some styling of its Chiswick-built full front body was shortly to influence the Board's design team when producing the first plan of the new bus.

Working from the brief description provided in the minutes of the Engineering Committee, it is possible to determine the original livery applied to the model of the vehicle before the initial colour scheme involving silver lines was adopted.

In January 1938, Rackham issued a statement implying that, as far as possible, priority would be given by AEC to the new chassis and that in review of the current situation, completion was thought possible by the middle of April. The latest items to occupy the minds of the design team were the cylindrical fuel tank with suitable length neck to permit use of the existing type of automatic filler installed in garages, and the RP brake adjuster mentioned in the first chapter.

During the first weeks of 1938, Durrant was required to provide a presentation regarding the proposed new bus on three separate occasions. The first took place on 3 January when he attended a meeting of the Engineering Committee using as a visual aid the model of the new bus based on the plan produced six weeks earlier.

The Committee requested the following revisions: (a) no commercial advertisement to be provided on the offside lower panel; (b) single silver bands to be provided above and below the lower windows in place of the double bands with consideration being given to lowering the side streamer advertisement; (c) the black beading in the upper deck to be carried continuously round the front of the bus and changed to silver lines. Previously distributed for discussion at the meeting was a submission by Durrant headed '1939 Double Deck Bus – Increased Cost'. Prefacing his report by stating that the final design was still being prepared, he recorded that improvements to be incorporated included those of appearance, performance and longevity. Such development had been the result of experimental work and a comprehensive study of the most suitable forms of body construction. Having sugared the pill, Durrant stated that the vehicle's cost would inevitably be increased, his estimate being £130 above the present price for the construction of an STL, which then stood at £1,500. The increase was due to the following:

1) Chassis
a) The provision of a larger engine incorporating more generous bearing surfaces resulting in longer life.
b) Incorporation of full air pressure brakes for the purpose of increasing the reserve of braking power, elimination of manual adjustment and a lighter operating pedal.
c) Rubber mounting of engine to prevent transmission of vibration to the body.
d) Air pressure servo of transmission to reduce driver's fatigue and improve the control mechanism of the vehicle.

The estimated additional capital cost in respect of the foregoing was £50.

2) Body
a) Improvement in construction with a view to a reduction in maintenance cost.
b) Improvement in interior finishing, including provision of a double skin roof for the upper deck.
c) Improvement in the design of wings and more extensive use of rubber, with a view to saving on maintenance costs.
d) Improved appearance resulting, to some extent, in more expensive work.
e) Improved ventilation and seating for driver's cab.

The estimated extra capital cost in respect of the foregoing was £80.

Durrant continued to make his case and estimated that in the likelihood of a reduction in fuel and engine maintenance costs, an annual saving of £41 per vehicle could be obtained from these items alone. In addition, the vehicle would be built with a view to increasing the interval between mechanical dock overhauls that would result in an eventual saving at garages although he was unable to place a figure on this amount. He reasoned that by the improved appearance of the new vehicle and the longer-lasting type of construction used for the body, its depreciation period could, if desired, be extended. In concluding his summary, the Chief Engineer reminded the meeting that approval had already been obtained for one experimental vehicle of the type described to have a short period of operation under service conditions before production commenced. The Committee accepted Durrant's report and requested that it should be submitted to a Chairman's meeting together with the model, once their modifications to its livery and advertisement positions had been completed.

The question of contracts was then debated and the Engineering Committee members agreed that the prototype vehicle would be perfected in conjunction with AEC in anticipation of orders for the production chassis being placed with the company.

Despite giving an initial blessing to the project, the Board's Chairman Lord Ashfield appears to have received little information about the experimental bus. Most correspondence on its design had been directed to his deputy, Frank Pick by Durrant who, on 27 January 1938, attended a Chairman's meeting with the revised model, its purpose again being to demonstrate general outline and proposed colour scheme. In approving the design of the new bus, those assembled requested further consideration be given to forward radiator design and the position of the rear platform window on the offside.

Some authorities have written that the existence of the platform window was to allow the conductor to indicate a right turn, a belief held by the author until the content of experiment S4599 was studied. Raised in the winter of 1936-37 at the request of A T Wilford (the Board's Chief Chemist), the experiment considered the ventilation of STL platforms following a suggestion that there should be a reduction in the discomfort of conductors caused by a collection of fumes from either the bus itself or surrounding vehicles in heavy traffic. The detailed tests were carried out under a variety of conditions, involving a sampling of the carbon dioxide levels contaminating the platform area. Although, in his conclusion written in February 1937, Wilford considered any additional ventilation of the platform was impracticable, he also believed such a facility desirable. However, a problem he foresaw was that an offside window, if kept permanently open in all weathers, would result in further complaints. In the outcome, a one-piece window that slid horizontally was fitted to the prototype body allowing the conductor to control the entry of fresh air.

Durrant was required to provide two statements for the meeting of the Board held on 3 February 1938. The first was entitled 'Programme of Rolling Stock – Buses and Coaches' and gave members a situation report regarding the delivery of the current bus building programme. At the time, three STL chassis were yet to be delivered by AEC and at Chiswick, ten STL bodies awaited construction. Durrant then confirmed that completion of these vehicles under Special Expenditure Requisition No G280 would bring to an end production of the existing design of double deck bus and, anticipating the new bus, further double deck vehicles would not be due for production until February 1939. The second statement was identical to that previously presented to the meetings of the Engineering Committee and Chairman in January, the Board then agreeing to adopt the report and in consequence the Chief Engineer's explanation that the cost of the new vehicle would be higher than that of an STL. Finally, and not to be outdone by the recommendations for changes in design requested at the previous meetings, the Board asked that consideration be given to a suggestion for having route numbers placed on the near- and offside upper front corners of the bus instead of the front roof route number box.

Durrant was later to report to the Engineering Committee that it was neither practical nor desirable to display route numbers as proposed by the Board. Instead, he suggested that a stencil containing the route number should be displayed on the nearside of the vehicle beneath the projecting front of the upper saloon forming the canopy above the engine compartment. The Committee approved the arrangement and requested a report be submitted to the Board.

AEC became the subject of criticism by Eric Ottaway when the JEC convened in late January over the preparation and design of new vehicles. At the meeting, he requested that some means should be adopted to ensure that new programmes were created from past specification lists produced by the Board and not those of AEC so that vehicles conformed to certain accepted London Transport features. By way of example, he stated that the cylinder head cover for the 10T10 engine had been produced by AEC in aluminium instead of 'electron' (a magnesium alloy) and the oil filler was the company's design and not of the type required by the Board. Ottaway believed that had the lists provided by London Transport been consulted, then such errors would not have arisen. George Robinson, Rackham's deputy, agreed to take relevant action.

In late February 1938, Ottaway informed the JEC that Leyland had asked him for a copy of the specification outlining the Board's future requirements for double-deck vehicles. Ottaway proposed that this should be prepared based around the performance sought by the Board for the new bus, although Rackham requested the specification be made available to him before it was passed to Leyland. Ottaway then turned his attention to the new chassis, then under construction at Southall, stating that the vehicle was unlikely to have achieved sufficient service mileage to show any minor problems before a decision became necessary regarding the building programme. Durrant again indicated that he did not wish to continue with the existing design of STL in 1939. Following discussion, it was considered that the material situation would remain sufficient for the new bus if the final specification was settled before the end of August. Up to this point, minor changes could be incorporated following experience gained with the prototype chassis. Consequently, the immediate release of jig and tool drawings was thought necessary to allow production to commence with minimum delay especially if, as thought, the order for the new buses could be placed by May.

A spanner was firmly inserted in the works by George Robinson in early March when he reported that AEC did not think it possible to produce the new chassis in quantity to meet LT delivery requirements. This situation had arisen due to extensive tool design demanded of the type although the first engines were currently undergoing road tests and he anticipated their availability for inspection very shortly. He therefore proposed that if the Board was to release an order for 100 STLs identical to the last batch, production of the 1939 double deck vehicle could follow immediately.

J H Bruce, representing the Board, agreed to assess the reaction of the Chiswick body shops to AEC's proposal, which would also be referred to Durrant. As a result, another STL chassis order was placed initially comprising 115 vehicles but subsequently increased by a further 17 for the Country department and, as the buses had an improved mechanical specification, they were coded 15STL16.

On 23 March 1938, Rackham, still referring to the new buses as '1939 Double Deck Vehicles, STL16' – more correctly 16STL – proposed that, in view of the volume of design questions to be discussed, special meetings should be convened. The JEC agreed to hold the first on 28 March, but no record of these meetings has been traced and for a time the new bus received little attention at full JEC meetings. The only reference was to endorse a decision that, prior to the mounting of the first body, every endeavour would be made to incorporate as many chassis production items as possible.

A number of many Special Expenditure Requisitions were approved by Board members attending a Chairman's Meeting held on 2 May 1938. The last to be considered referred to Requisition No G316 that amounted to £3,750 for the purchase of one AEC 'RT' chassis and for the building of one special double deck body for fitting to this chassis. This is the first reference to the code RT found in official records. The figure quoted for the chassis was £250 above the estimate placed on its construction by AEC nine months earlier. A rider to the minute requested 'Authority to Withdraw Redundant Assets (AWRA) Advice No G5/5 covering one Leyland TD Double Deck Bus (Central) at Walthamstow Garage'. This was also approved.

(c) Requisition of No. G. 316, amounting to £3,750, for the purchase of 1 A.E.C 'RT' chassis with oil engine and fluid transmission and for the building of one special double deck body for fitting to this chassis.

APPROVED. To be charged as to Capital Account   £1,875
          As to Maintenance Reserve Account   £1,875

This extract from a Chairman's meeting held on 2 May 1938 illustrates the first recorded use of the code RT, but only to describe the AEC chassis.

The significance of the letters RT has been the source of discussion among many authorities. A possibility that came to light during the research for this book is that the code could derive from a series of 'programme' codes used by AEC for its products. As examples, the final pre-war batch of STL chassis (15STL) was given the AEC programme code R.N. and the code R.S. was allocated on 8th February 1938 for some ship engineering parts. It would therefore appear quite possible that the code R.T. was initially allocated by AEC to the construction of the prototype chassis and later withdrawn when it was realised that the JEC experiment number would suffice. Although this code was allocated, or reallocated perhaps, in July 1938 to an order for 300 oil engines for LT type buses, there are two instances in JEC minutes about the new bus that refer to 'Programme R.T.', a code that may, without too much thinking, have been adopted by the people at Chiswick. The fact that the letters could also stand for Regent Type may just be a coincidence.

It should be placed on record here that, while he held his appointment with London Transport, A A M Durrant would not permit the term "diesel" to be used and the description "oil engine" remained in the vocabulary of the operator for some considerable time. Durrant's approved terminology is used throughout this book.

RT 1's chassis was completed at Southall on 16 May 1938 and was received at Chiswick exactly one week later. On the delivery note is recorded 'experimental chassis' against the heading reserved for model type, while S4810, the number of the experiment allocated to the project, appears before the chassis number O6616749. Engine No.3 is shown as having been fitted as number LH 805/1 for which experiment S4754 had been raised. The first entry on the vehicle's log card is dated 6 June 1938 next to which is written 'chassis', indicating its receipt at Chiswick, the dissimilarity between this date and that on the delivery note giving grounds for belief that the chassis was returned to Southall for two weeks for modification before its acceptance by the Board.

The chassis design for the RT differed from previous AEC types although it demonstrated a family likeness in side elevation by having a high front, low centre, usual style of wheel arch and low straight rear. However, when viewed from above, starting from the rear, the frame was parallel until approximately the centre of its length, where it tapered slightly to a position near the flywheel where parallel construction resumed to the front dumb irons. This contrasted with previous designs that saw the chassis frame running parallel from the rear to a point roughly under the front seats where it tapered to the front.

A specially shaped cross-member was bolted between the inner sides of the dumb irons at the top of which an encased circular rubber mounting of significant density provided support for the front of the engine. A further four cross-members were located along the chassis, the first of these carrying a rear rubber mounting assembly for the engine and a bracket for the compressor and dynamo; the second carried the gearbox and the front end of the silencer, the third the rear wheel air pressure brake cylinders and the rearmost the road spring shackle brackets. A single spacing bar was located to the rear of the frame extension, to which the platform was attached.

During May 1938, Eric Ottaway visited Berlin. He reported that the most outstanding feature on German vehicles was the use of compressed air. He was most impressed that the air braking of vehicles on which he had travelled was superior to that generally available in the United Kingdom. Ottaway was pleased to place on record that from his observations the Board's approach was justified in standardising on compressed air equipment for future designs. However, he doubted whether any of the braking layouts he saw in Germany were as complete as the system adopted for the prototype chassis, no system having been found there that provided compressed air brakes with complete compensation and fully automatic adjustment.

Compressed air was also used on the RT for gear changing. The system gave a reduction in the usual physical effort required, the gear change pedal being heavy enough for accurate control. The gear lever was sited on the steering column working in a gate and used to pre-select the required gear in conjunction with the fluid flywheel. Previously compressed air had mainly been used for the brakes on trolleybuses and a handful of experimental STLs, while the gearbox of the Leyland TF was also pneumatically operated but the unit differed considerably from that fitted to the RT chassis. An innovative use was also made of the air supply in powering the RP chassis lubrication system, the circuits for which were activated by the brake pedal.

The Dodson body (incorrectly described as being of Leyland manufacture on the vehicle's log card) from TD 111 was fitted to the prototype chassis on 1 July 1938; the resulting vehicle, given the number ST 1140, was licensed on 7 July at the rate of £45 7s 3d. A certificate of fitness for five years was issued on 8 July and the vehicle transferred to Hanwell garage five days later. Metropolitan Stage Carriage plate 9149N was also allocated to the vehicle, the RT chassis being the only member of the class to receive such identification, their issuing for motor buses having fallen into disuse by the time the production batch was being built. In addition to the method of mounting, some modification to the Dodson body was required before it could be fitted to the prototype chassis. This consisted mainly of traps set in the lower deck floor for the inspection and maintenance of the running units; space for the two 12V batteries was made beneath the staircase. Adaptations to the offside included access through the safety rails to the air tank for the RP lubricator and a cab access step above which was installed a battery booster socket. Some repanelling was necessary on the offside to remove access to the fuel tank filler, such provision having to be made on the nearside. In view of the lower

Still in existence among the archives held by TfL at Acton Depot is a ledger detailing daily changes to the bus fleet. On 12 July 1938, the number of licensed buses stood at 5113, this figure being maintained the following day when an STL was deducted from the total and a new vehicle listed in a column headed "RT" – using the correct description for the prototype chassis. In addition to the remodelling of the front end of the Dodson body from TD 111 to suit the lower AEC radiator, other noticeable changes included provision for the fuel filler on the nearside of the vehicle, a battery booster socket above the driver's step and an access point for the RP lubricator oil tank through the lifeguard rails.

position of the radiator, some adaptation of the cab front was necessary although this failed to alter conspicuously the outward appearance of the bus.

The proximity of Hanwell garage to AEC's Southall works made it an ideal base for ST 1140 during the six-month period when the new RT chassis was being evaluated. In the absence from LT's archives of experiment numbers S4810 (chassis) and S4754 (engine) little is known of the results achieved when the vehicle occasionally ran in service on route 18C. A recently discovered document shows the vehicle running on route 18C as HW 7 covering ten return journeys on Monday to Friday between Hanwell and Wembley from 7.32am to 6.52pm, thirteen return journeys on Saturday as HW 4 from 7.24am to 12.15am and six return journeys on Sunday as HW 3 between Hanwell and Kings Cross from 8.35am and 12.2am. One record found was the result of an experiment conducted by AEC under the reference A1090 – a bench test – whose report refers to the adaptation of the 8.8 litre engine to replicate the performance of a 9.6 litre engine to gain performance data and to settle in advance as many details as possible regarding the combustion chamber and injection equipment. However, adaptations to replicate the size of the new engine, including the provision of hastily manufactured pistons, resulted in several engine seizures and, after considerable modification, excessive noise became a problem. There had been some expectation that difficulties would be encountered with the application of a pot type combustion chamber to an engine of different capacity, and as a result, several attempts were made to produce some meaningful data. A new set of pistons was subsequently made and a new block machined and fitted. In this form, no further seizures occurred and the noise from the engine equated well with that of an 8.8 litre unit.

ST 1140 was withdrawn on 31 December 1938, the Dodson body then being removed. All the trials escaped the attention of the technical press. Little remains of the experiments, save for the few scant references above and two official but uncaptioned photographs, to provide us with any record of the testing of an extremely revolutionary chassis.

Although there was significant similarity between the first general arrangement plan produced in 1937 for the 1939 double deck vehicle and the prototype, some changes were still to be made supplemental to those put forward by the various committees. Among the more obvious was the remodelling of the cab to allow for the installation of a sliding door, the upper edge of its window frame providing a link to the profile as originally proposed; in consequence, the small window to the rear nearside of the cab was deleted. Although not entirely uncommon, most motor bus types operating in the capital did not have the luxury of a cab door, and when fitted such examples opened outwards; the RT's sliding cab door evolved as a result of space limitations in garages. The bonnet area, reminiscent of the 10T10, underwent revision which resulted in the fleet number plate being placed centrally. Other variations included a reversal of the rear destination panel, and the replacement, using a single sliding pane, of the two-piece staircase window. However, a record has yet to surface regarding the more forward placing of the fleetname, the new site never becoming a serious contender for adoption on the RT. The London Transport fleetname had been the subject of experiment S4182, which commenced in mid-June 1935, using transfers provided by H M Stevenson and Son Ltd. These were applied using bronze powder instead of aluminium powder then used for transfers from the Board's usual supplier. According to the report, the appearance of the fleetname became more distinctive by appearing darker in colour. Eric Ottaway approved Stevenson as supplier.

When first used on the RT the fleetname transfers were centrally applied to the panels beneath the second and third bay windows, which resulted in the 'T' of Transport appearing slightly to the left of the flat steel vertical beading dividing the panels. This practice remained a standard feature of the 2RT2 until late in their existence. On post-war variants, this letter was applied so that its vertical bar was aligned with the steel beading, which led to some early problems, and additional supplies of the letter had to be made available to replace those damaged by movement of the body.

By 1939, the construction of passenger vehicle bodies had been the subject of much development. The original principles had been based on the technique of the carriage builder, which persisted until shortly after the the First World War when the flitched composite type of body was introduced. This form of construction employed a timber framework strengthened by the insertion of steel flitches or plates; the panelling, either plywood or sheet aluminium was then attached to the structure. Experiment S3506 had been conducted in May 1934 to determine the effects of flitching body pillars which showed a strength reduction of 32% when their central steel flitch plate was omitted. Service requirements necessitated local bracing and eventually a timber structure was evolved that comprised tenon and half-lapped joints at such places as the pillar feet and the waist and cant rails but still strengthened by the addition of metal brackets and other especially produced metalwork.

In 1930, all-metal bodies made their appearance and initially this style of body consisted of a metal framework to which panels and floors were riveted. However, this form of construction was found to produce a noisier bus and deemed unsuitable for maintenance purposes by operating companies, which favoured the use of timber and woodscrews, largely due to cheapness of repair and the replacement of panels that had suffered minor damage. In consequence, a modified form of all-metal construction was introduced, notably by Metro-Cammell, that employed a metal framework to which the inner panels below the waist rails were riveted to form the necessary truss plates. The framework was loaded with timber so that the panelling and fittings could be attached in the orthodox manner. This form of construction proved very satisfactory and was extensively used and copied. Since much timber was used purely for the purpose of fastenings and attachments the result was a heavier body than for the composite form of construction. To solve the problem of increased weight, an improved form of assembly was developed by the Board for its single and double deck buses. This was an extension of the previous composite form of construction and was seen as a compromise between the all-metal and the earlier types. Eliminated was the use of normal tenon and half-lapped joints, their place taken by special forms of metal bracketing on which the stress was taken by interlocking indentations. The various plates and brackets were bolted wherever possible to the framework and punch countersinking was widely used to ensure a satisfactory grip of the timber parts of the body.

The bodies built for RT 1 and the 2RT2 vehicles were of composite construction, that of the prototype hardly differing from the production vehicles; many of the plans produced for the 2RT2 were based on those drawn for the first body. One significant variation was in the type of waist rail immediately below the lower deck windows to which the top fixing lug of each transverse seat frame was bolted. In the construction of the RT2 bodies, the rail was produced with weight reduction/strengthening holes, replacing one of narrower section used in the assembly of the first body. The aircraft industry may well have influenced the design of the newer rail, since components of a similar but lighter type were, by then, an integral part of airframes such as that of the Supermarine Spitfire.

All metal welded girder construction was used in the fabrication of the front bulkhead within which a new concept of positive dowel location was employed to ensure parallelism of the body with the chassis. Perforated panels for sound absorption were an integral part of this assembly that gave support to the rear of the cab and the nearside wing assembly. An identical bulkhead was used in the production vehicles, additional strengthening coming later. Some authorities conclude that the construction of the prototype body made simpler its mounting on the first RT chassis, the truncating of which occurred following the removal of the body from TD 111. The platform framing for the prototype body differed from the production batch; made more apparent by the first drawings produced for the RT2 body being of this area.

As we have seen, any change in the construction of the Board's buses was invariably the subject of intensive testing and results from experiment S5065 were undertaken in the design of RT 1's platform before any departures from accepted principles. Raised in the spring of 1938, the experiment first assumed that the tail end of a bus chassis gave some measure of support to the platform and rear of the body. In view of the possibility that, at some future date, buses would be designed without a platform fixing to chassis, the Technical Officer's team at Chiswick decided to ascertain the effects of removing all fixings and packing bolts. Under these conditions, the whole of the loading stresses were absorbed in the rear of the body and the platform with no assistance being provided by the chassis extension.

STL 2463 (with body number 17886) was first licensed on 10 January 1938 and after a period of four months in service was withdrawn for the experiment. In each of the tests, apparatus consisting of two levers was used; one connected to the chassis frame, the other to the platform. Pointers were attached to the ends of the levers, these marking on a card the relative movement of the platform and chassis. Four tests were conducted, for the first the unladen STL, but with platform still clipped to the chassis, was driven around the Chiswick works test track and subjected to shock bumping and body rolling. The second test was similar to the first although on this occasion, the STL carried a load of 24 persons situated on the staircase, platform and rear end of the upper saloon. For the third and fourth tests, all platform support, packings and fixing bolts were removed, which allowed the chassis to flex independently from the platform, and the bus subjected to the same loading conditions as in the first and second tests.

From the results, it was discovered that when the platform and chassis were bolted together, the packings tended to force the body away from the chassis. Upon disconnection, however, the platform was able to adopt its natural shape. While no great deflection was encountered on the platform when unclipped, the chassis extension did provide some slight measure of support. In this state, the body was given more freedom to flex during cornering. There can be little doubt that the experiment was being conducted in anticipation of future designs. The report's final recommendation at the end of October 1938 requested that no further action be taken until the STL body had received an extended service period and inspected for any structural movement or breakages. Thereafter, should no defects be found, the question of deleting chassis extensions would be seriously considered. The tail was separated from the prototype chassis in the intervening months following the removal of the Dodson body and the mounting of the Chiswick-built body. The vehicle's log card records the change but fails to provide a date when surgery took place. A further reason given for the reduction in length considered the effect of the chassis frame becoming distorted should a rear end collision occur.

In December, J W Wicks confirmed that Chiswick had dispatched to Southall a pre-select gearbox for the new vehicle, its chassis having been returned to Southall following the testing period. During January 1939, Ottaway asked that AEC loan Chiswick an example of the engine developed for the RT, to be supplied complete with all ancillary drives and before the delivery of the modified prototype chassis. The new engine was numbered A185. The A185 was a 9.6 litre 6-cylinder engine of advanced design. The Joint Experimental Committee had agreed that a pot type combustion chamber should be installed, which effectively reduced the mechanical and thermal losses formerly experienced with earlier engines. Many features were included resulting from the combined experience of AEC and the LPTB in the manufacture and operation of oil engines although there was an important departure from the draft specification presented to the AEC directors in October 1937. This resulted in the installation of a shaft on the offside of the engine to drive the air compressor and dynamo, an innovation that would cause a number of problems, many experienced soon after the first of the new vehicles entered service.

This photograph of the prototype chassis is dated 24 March 1939, just three days before the first RT body was mounted. Absent from the chassis is the temporary screen that used the same mounting points for the front bulkhead. To the screen were fitted a seat and the auxiliary fuel tank, which in this view appears precariously supported above the engine.

These two views were taken at Chiswick between 27 and 29 March 1939. During this short period, a painter added an additional coloured band between the upper and lower deck windows on one side of the vehicle only, which was then driven to Willesden Garage on 30 March for inspection by Durrant and Frank Pick. Both gentlemen agreed to adopt the colour scheme requiring a side band of light colour, although no mention is made in the official records regarding the change in the colour of the roof from silver to red. During their deliberations, Pick and Durrant also decided that the window on the stairs on the offside should be omitted. The term "signalling window" does not appear. Rawlings Manufacturing Co was contracted to provide the half drop lights, the company's PYP window range differing from the Hallam, Sleigh & Cheston examples found on the production vehicles. The forward facing PYP half drops on both decks had central winding handles, those fitted to the RT2s being positioned towards the outer edge. The body number for RT 1 was 18246, this number falling between those built for T 601 (18245) and T 609 (18247) both taken into LT stock on 8 July 1938.

Taken into account during the construction of the body for RT 1 was the Engineering Committee's request of January 1938 for the livery to include a series of horizontal silver lines. This was achieved by fixing in the positions so identified, fluted aluminium beading (i.e. with a concave centre) the whole of which would be polished to produce the desired effect. Also subjected to similar treatment was the flat, inverted horseshoe beading that bordered the nearside fuel tank filler. The roof was finished in aluminium, as were the driving mirror frames. From photographic evidence, it can be ascertained that, upon leaving the Chiswick paint shop, no variation existed in finish on each side of the vehicle. Yet when the vehicle was viewed by Pick and Durrant at Willesden garage on 30 March 1939, a clerk later recorded that the bus had on either side between the lower and upper deck windows alternative schemes of coloured bands for their consideration. After inspecting the prototype, Pick and Durrant approved the general arrangement of RT 1 for production, subject to omission of the offside window on the stairs and the adoption of a light coloured side band, presumably in off-white.

The only conclusion that can be drawn from the foregoing is that one side of the prototype was painted to demonstrate a livery that included a coloured inter-deck dividing band. Whether all horizontal beading on this side was painted to match the adjacent areas is unrecorded in similar circumstance to the absence of any decision on the colour of the roof. Nevertheless, RT 1 was repainted as requested and made ready for the official photographer the following month, sporting a livery that it would retain until its first overhaul. Also parked on 30 March in Willesden garage awaiting Pick and Durrant's comments were two TF coaches in alternative colour schemes. History does not record the fleet number of one, but the darker green colour applied to TF 27c was approved for adoption as standard for Green Line.

Despite RT 1 having been extensively photographed during April outside Orford Hall (later St Michael's Convent) on Ham Common, another area of the bus's design still required approval: the position of route numbers. At its meeting held on 22 May 1939 the Works Committee approved all points with the exception of the offside and under-canopy route number stencils. For the former, two alternative locations were on offer, one making use of the small staircase window, the continuance of which had been rejected by Pick and Durrant; the other was set between the small window and the lower deck windows with advertisement space to its rear. The latter position was approved subject to a report from the Chief Commercial Officer regarding the value of an advertising space on the rear offside panel. In the absence of any filed report, it must be assumed that the Chief Commercial Officer was not in favour of the suggestion. Yet when the production batch appeared the offside route number stencil was placed immediately adjacent to the rear saloon window failing to replicate the more central position selected for RT 1.

The new vehicle underwent some changes in seating before its presentation to the press in July 1939. When officially photographed the previous April, the Dunlopillo seat cushions and squabs were covered in green moquette of a design previously selected for use on STLs. However, the Board decided that a new style of moquette should be used to trim the bus, using green, brown and black in a regular pattern divided by red strands. In keeping with current practice, both components of the double transverse seats were produced with blocked leather ends, the back of the squab being covered in green rexine. On 6 July 1939, RT 1's seating capacity was reduced from 56 to 55 by the removal of the only freestanding seat on the bus situated on the upper deck; four-legged frame construction was necessary here, the interior casing of the side blind box preventing the use of a lower seat-fixing bracket (known as a skate). A single seat was substituted, the change made necessary in order to reduce the overall weight of the vehicle, this being slightly above the 10½ tons gross laden weight restriction. The unladen weight of the vehicle was recorded on 6 July as 6t 15cwt 3q.

One week later, RT 1 met the press at Aldwych, articles appearing in some national daily papers the following day. The Board's staff magazine *Pennyfare* and the *AEC Gazette* – the company's in-house journal – sent reporters, both making use of the press handouts provided by the Public Relations Officer. An innovation that caught the eye of the AEC reporter was the extension on the nearside bulkhead that had been designed to carry a rubber wing. Having been incorporated in the styling of the 10T10 and tested on STL 2464, the wing extension became the subject of a short exchange between AEC and the Board, the latter thinking that this component formed part of the chassis.

On 1 June 1939, Durrant wrote to Pick to advise him that the cost for building RT 1 had exceeded its budget, which had been set on 5 August 1937. The construction of the chassis at a cost of £3,500 had been agreed, the Board paying £1,000 to AEC, each then expected to take a half share in the remaining balance (i.e. £1,250). Durrant then stated that when all the charges were received from AEC, the Board's share would be £2,076 or £826 more than had been allowed under Special Expenditure Requisition G316 to which the cost of the project had been allocated. The delay in calculating the over-expenditure was the fault of AEC, the company having incorrectly allocated to the Board only half the cost of an experiment costing £1,000 instead of the whole amount. Durrant suggested that, as the budgeted Experimental Account for year ending 30 June 1939 was underspent by £1,000, over-expenditure on RT 1 could be charged to that account and the Board in due course agreed.

During its outing on 13 July 1939, RT 1 was driven from Aldwych to the Spaniards Inn situated on Spaniards Road, Hampstead. The absence of the kerb guide on the nearside front wing is apparent together with the siting of the under-canopy route number, opposition to which led to a spring-loaded stencil holder on the RT2 bodies. During discussions regarding the offside stencil plate, a suggestion was made for its deletion in favour of the route number being displayed in the platform window.

Preparations for a Classic

At the meeting of the Board's Engineering Committee held in September 1938, Durrant sought authority to place an immediate order with AEC for 150 RT chassis following the STL building programme scheduled for completion in September 1939. He intimated that such action was necessary in view of the length of time before delivery of the vehicles could commence and in consequence, the Committee agreed that a Special Expenditure Requisition would be submitted without delay. Eric Ottaway advised the Joint Engineering Committee of the order during its meeting on 6 October 1938, gaining an assurance from G J Rackham work would soon commence on the preparation of the necessary drawings and lists required for tooling. Specification 9638 was allocated to the project and Ottaway confirmed that the Board would arrange for its swift completion; unfortunately, a copy of this document appears not to have been archived. However, when produced, the document would have set down in detail the manufacturing and finishing processes for the chassis frame and its associated running units together with comprehensive construction techniques for the body. AEC allocated Programme SY to the order for 150 chassis.

At a Chairman's meeting held on 27 October 1938, Special Expenditure Requisition G325 was approved under the heading Bus and Coach Rolling Stock Programme 1939/1940, which comprised: 17 STL chassis fitted with 115mm bore oil engines, 338 RT chassis fitted with 115mm bore oil engines, 17 STL double deck bodies and 341 RT double deck bodies (including 3 spares).

It was not until 17 May 1939 that information regarding the increase in number of chassis was conveyed to the JEC, which immediately requested the Board issue a variation sheet to cover the programme's extension by 188 chassis, for which AEC allocated the programme code UB.

Unlike the separate meetings convened by the JEC to consider the first RT, production vehicles were openly discussed at the fortnightly meetings and fortunately, one set of minutes survives. At the meeting held on 19 October 1938, Ottaway called for one complete chassis and a gearbox be supplied to the Board ahead of the manufacturing schedule. His request went unfulfilled and the prototype remained the only example in the Board's possession until the delivery to Chiswick of the chassis for RT 15 and RT 23 some twelve months later.

Some concern by the Board still centred on the design of the A185 engine and consideration was being given to using pistons of the Leyland type. This situation was not resolved until mid-May 1939 when a decision was made to use pistons produced to an AEC design by Specialloid Ltd of North Finchley. An assurance was requested from AEC that there would be no recurrence of the recent faults experienced with the cylinder block of the 10T10 A180 engines. The company stated that a revision in design had eradicated the problem.

Although in January 1939 delivery was some months away, an experiment was proposed by the JEC that called for the fitting of Miller semi-automatic gear changing equipment to twelve RTs for extended service trials but these were never undertaken. An earlier test with a unit fitted to STL 760 had been conducted but it was not until May 1939 that Durrant submitted a report in which he recommended that the system should be adopted following a satisfactory conclusion of the earlier tests.

In February 1939, the dynamo specified for the chassis was of CAV Bosch manufacture for which was placed an order for 150. In late March, Ottaway emphasised the urgent need for AEC to supply a copy of the chassis arrangement for the coachbuilders at Chiswick and during early April discussion centred on the overall weight of the chassis, AEC later stating that it would make every effort not to exceed 3t 15cwt 2qrs.

Some early concerns were registered regarding the compressed air system when Ottaway recommended at the mid-May 1939 meeting, the provision of an auxiliary air supply tank to operate the gearbox in the event of an emergency. Contact with Clayton Dewandre was suggested but ahead of the company's response, Ottaway promoted a scheme whereby an auxiliary tank was fitted to the chassis side member. The adaptation was subsequently approved by Clayton Dewandre and the company was requested to supply the additional component.

The dynamo drive came under scrutiny in June 1939, and alterations made to its design while a variation was made to the original specification regarding the cylinder head air intake that would be the subject of swift modification following the first vehicles' entry into service. An adjustment to the chassis at this time reduced its overall length by 12mm to suit body requirements, the completed bus having a turning circle of 54 feet 4 inches, improving on the anticipated 56 feet.

Although programme UB that had been raised by AEC might be seen as an extension to the original order, each element of the additional 188 chassis required release by the Board and, in consequence, the first four components were approved at the end of June although many remained in abeyance. Changes in specification continued to be made to the original 150 chassis and under consideration at this time was the means of swift indication to the driver of a loss of air pressure. On earlier vehicles so equipped, a warning lamp was fitted below the speedometer and shared its casing, but the JEC agreed that either a gauge or an apparatus similar to the indicators fitted to trolleybuses would be more appropriate. By the end of July, agreement had been reached for the installation of a unit manufactured by the Westinghouse Brake and Signal Company, its stop flag falling into the driver's line of vision when air pressure was lost. The device, which also illuminated a warning lamp, was then included as part of the body.

While the Joint Experimental Committee dealt with items that mainly concerned chassis development, the Board's Main Technical Committee authorised experiments that would have an effect on bodywork.

During the early part of 1937, some difficulties were experienced in obtaining supplies of aluminium and steel sheeting, due mainly to a significant increase in aircraft construction. In view of the situation becoming more serious, experiment S4739 was opened to consider the use of alternative materials. Calculations had found that in the event of an acute shortage of sheet metal, it might prove simpler to obtain stocks of plywood and in consequence, it was decided to undertake some service experience with buses fitted with birch and gaboon plywood panels. Plywood exterior panels had been used as standard in the manufacture of bodies for K and S type buses but the significant movement of their bodies allowed moisture to penetrate, and a change to steel panels occurred upon introduction of the NS.

The body framework of the STL was far more rigid in design reducing greatly the movement that had allowed water to seep into the wooden panels fitted to the earlier types. Before their entry into service in May and June 1937, the bodies of two STL14 bodies, STLs 1915 and 1939, were clad with gaboon and birch 4mm plywood panels in order to gain service experience. From the tests, birch was found the weightier although stronger in tension and compression than gaboon. Both materials were lighter than aluminium and considerably cheaper. Plywood could only used in such positions as flat surfaces and those with slight curvature; excluded were areas such as the rear corner, cab, upper deck front and roof.

Following two years in service, the results of the experiment found that if aluminium or steel sheeting became unobtainable, birch and gaboon plywood panelling would be suitable. Experience indicated that plywood gave better results for lower deck work if fitted to a sideframe with only a gradual contour such as on the STD and RT. The cost of partly cladding a bus in 17swg (1.422mm) aluminium sheeting amounted to £16 14s, in gaboon plywood £4 4s and in birch £1 17s.

The availability of aluminium to London Transport became more acute. By 3 November 1939, Frank Pick sent a memorandum to G F Sinclair, who had recently become the Board's Chief Engineer (Trams and Trolleybuses), regarding supply of the metal. Pick noted that Sinclair had been unable to secure the supplies he required to complete the construction of an additional 50 trolleybuses and suggested he consulted his colleagues, especially A A M Durrant and Graff Baker, Chief Mechanical Engineer (Railways), both of whom held reserve stocks of scrap aluminium.

A shortage of specialised metals began to have an effect on the design of seat frames used in the Board's vehicles and in January 1937, the Main Technical Committee commissioned experiment S4596 to report on the construction of transverse tubular seats. When the report was written, extreme difficulty was being experienced in obtaining supplies of MG7 and Hinduminium – both being aluminium alloys, the former introduced to the aircraft industry in 1931 and the latter into motor engineering by the Armstrong Siddeley Company. Tubing made from these alloys was used in the construction of seats as fitted to STL vehicles, and it was decided to review the whole question of design in an attempt to create an alternative that would be less affected by lack of supplies and probably cheaper to manufacture. The new style of seat that evolved had a polished finish for the top rails manufactured from either of the two mentioned alloys and a gangway side rail in yet another aluminium alloy known as Birmabright; the remainder of the frame was of painted or stove enamelled steel tube.

A product known as spiral Doverite was introduced during mid-1936 following complaints from conductors that their hands became blackened due to their frequent use of the aluminium handrails. Although no grounds for the complaint could be established when tests were carried out under experiment S4280, spiral Doverite was used to cover the area of handrails most often grasped with a result that the material was eventually introduced throughout the motor bus fleet. However, further experiments in December 1936 and April 1937 (S4730 and S4647) found 27 STLs fitted with leather covered handrails and stanchions; the test was deemed unsatisfactory.

The Board's buses were the subject of experiment S4334, under the title of Accident Prevention Test Equipment, which concluded in September 1938. The project arose from discussions held in late 1935 with the Operating Manager's Department in an endeavour to reduce the number of mishaps then prevalent in boarding and alighting accidents, collisions and falls on buses. Therefore 25 vehicles of the STL11 type were equipped with experimental features and arrangements made for any accidents in which they were involved to be compared with 25 standard vehicles. All 50 buses were allocated to Chelverton Road garage and, for direct comparison, they were used on routes 22 and 39. It was to route 22 that RT 1 was first allocated in August 1939.

All vehicles tested were fitted with three items: a repositioned bell push on the rear frame corner pillar, an additional driver's mirror on the nearside front corner pillar and two additional stanchions in the lower deck. Additionally the platform nosing was of a special type, nine buses being fitted with material of Ferodo manufacture, the remaining 16 with black Jay Bee edging.

Of the items installed, the Traffic Committee sanctioned the fitting of the additional stanchions and a driver's mirror to all new and existing vehicles. The thinking behind the repositioned bell push was to ensure that the conductor would automatically face the rear of the bus when giving the starting signal and thus reduce the number of accidents

Perhaps the most exceptional set of photographs to come into the author's possession during the compilation of this book are those that show RT 1 operating on route 22 during the late summer of 1939. All views were taken within the vicinity of Holborn Viaduct and Newgate Street. The first view shows the vehicle standing adjacent to the church of St Sepulchre-without-Newgate with buildings on Holborn Viaduct in the background (now demolished). The second view shows the vehicle as it enters Newgate Street. The rear three quarters view has the vehicle crossing the junction with Giltspur Street and Old Bailey with the Viaduct Tavern ahead. The bus continues to display the same exterior advertisements as applied when first officially photographed in its approved livery with the exception of that for Bisto beneath the rear platform window which has been replaced with an example extolling the virtues of Cerebos Salt. A dent in the front dome on the nearside and the use of the ventilator above the front screen are of interest.

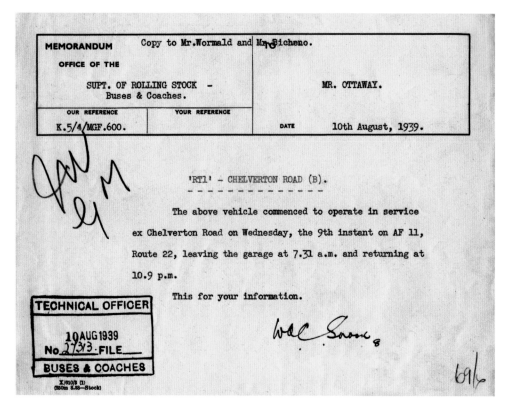

'RT1' – CHELVERTON ROAD (B).
– – – – – – – – – – – – – – – – –

The above vehicle commenced to operate in service
ex Chelverton Road on Wednesday, the 9th instant on AF 11,
Route 22, leaving the garage at 7.31 a.m. and returning at
10.9 p.m.

This for your information.

TECHNICAL OFFICER
10 AUG 1939
No.2733 . FILE___
BUSES & COACHES
X/610/3 (1)
(250m 8.38—Stock)

An internal memo recording the historic entry into service of RT 1 on 9th August 1939.

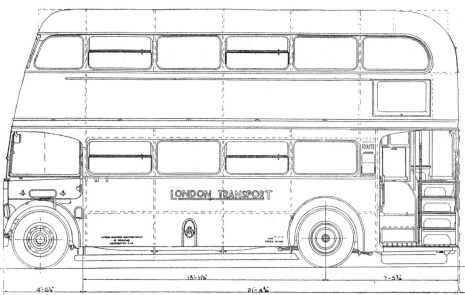

LONDON TRANSPORT

Some of the styling of RT 1 not perpetuated on the 2RT2s can be determined in this general arrangement plan. Most noticeable are the lack of rearward sweep to the wings, the deletion of the roof ventilator and the absence of an additional half-light on the upper deck. However, the edge of the canopy below the dividing band became deeper than that of the prototype and, in the absence of the minutes from meetings of the Bodywork Sub-Committee, the rationale behind this change remains unrecorded. The first RTs uniquely carried a nearside route number stencil and an angled mud flap beneath the platform.

suffered by intending passengers approaching from this direction; it was not adopted. The platform nosings were removed soon after their introduction due to a high rate of wear and a further experiment (S4226) undertaken at Hendon Garage using 25 STDs to which were fitted a non-slip and harder-wearing product known as pliable impregnated carborundum. A similar material known as Adamite was specified for the production RTs.

Rubber nearside front wings reappeared in early 1937 following negotiations with the Dunlop Rubber Company which produced a composite steel and rubber wing that was tested on an STL; all other wings fitted to the body had previously been produced in the same material. After some fifteen months in service (experiment S4835), the metal section of the wing had fractured necessitating its slight redesign. Events now overtook this testing and experiment S5054 was issued by the Main Technical Committee to report on the economics of rubber wings fitted to the Board's buses and coaches.

When a new vehicle was being planned, wings made from the more flexible material would be considered, the decision made simpler if those of an existing design were found compatible. Should the specification call for a new shaped wing, the cost of mould manufacture would be taken into account before the use of rubber was confirmed. A recent example of this had arisen when plans for the 10T10 were being produced and it was shown that the cost of the body would be reduced if rubber wings were made and fitted in lieu of metal. In consequence, the new RTs were so equipped.

On 8 August 1939, a memorandum produced by Durrant regarding the capital cost of new buses was the subject of his meeting with Pick. Durrant reported that detailed consideration had been given to whether it would be more economical to build buses to a cheaper standard than at present and run them for a shorter life. The conclusion reached was that such a course would be less economical than the present system. The memorandum set out the main items that had contributed in recent years towards the additional cost of new buses and Durrant suggested that it might be worthwhile to build an experimental vehicle on as cheap a basis as possible at some sacrifice to the present standards of luxury and performance. Immediately arising from their discussions, Pick and Durrant agreed that once the work in the Chiswick drawing office on the RT had been completed, its styling should be carefully analysed in detail. A full examination of the cost of the vehicle was to be undertaken and a report then submitted regarding the proposals of design staff for lowering the cost.

The majority of the plans for the body were produced during June and July 1939, the work being given the series reference 3571. Most of those produced before Durrant's meeting with Pick related to the actual framework of the vehicle and show no signs of major revision. Later plans reflect the style of finishing that would be applied to the vehicle and in these, departures were made from the prototype body presumably to address the request for cheapening. Items such as removal of the rearward flair of the wings, deletion of the ventilator above the front windscreen and remodelling of the driver's door were the most noticeable. Other changes deleted an opening window from the nearside of the upper deck, and the lock on the air intake grill above the upper deck front windows. The unique fluted horizontal beading was not perpetuated, being replaced with a half round moulding which, according to the plan, was to be manufactured in wood as an alternative to drawn aluminium section. The front dome on the prototype was redesigned for the RT2 bodies.

The efficiency of the Ashanco roof ventilator was the subject of experiment S5353 undertaken in May 1939 by a team of examiners who used smoke from a drain tester to ascertain how quickly the upper deck cleared. The STL provided for the experiment was driven forward at 25mph with the upper deck windows closed and the front bulkhead ventilator unlocked. Two tests were conducted, the first with the Ashanco unit open, the second with it blocked by paper. In both cases, the majority of the smoke cleared via the stairway and as a result, no recommendation could be made for including the roof ventilator as part of the 2RT2 specification.

An omission from the prototype body was a gutter above the rear upper deck emergency exit, which in order to prevent ingress of water was soon added to the RT2 body specification. By way of contrast, the canopy valance on the production bodies was extended below the central band, that of RT 1 being almost insignificant.

31

War and Cancellation

As the situation in Europe worsened, plans were formulated across the Country in an attempt to cope with every foreseeable eventuality that could arise from aerial bombardment. The Board's Air Raid Precautions Committee had begun meeting in early 1937, yet it was not until that fateful first Sunday in September 1939 that its emergency plans became a reality. One of a number of booklets giving directions to vehicle operators was entitled 'Wartime Lighting Restrictions – Lights Carried by Road Vehicles'. Its introductory paragraph containing the following: ' ... no lamps, other than the red rear or stop lamps and direction indicators and white obligatory lamps and masked headlamp may be used on the outside of any vehicle'. The booklet qualifies the last item listed by stating that: 'one headlamp (i.e. a lamp exceeding a power of 7 watts) may be used provided that the light is white and it has been fitted with a mask. In situations where two headlamps are fitted, the bulb should be removed from that on the offside'. The regulation regarding headlamps had an immediate effect on the design of the RT, in which the offside headlamp was deleted from its specification. The decision is questionable, as should the headlamp have been fitted, the Government's statutory requirements could have been met by simply removing the bulb.

Blackout, when used to describe the drastic reduction in after-dark lighting during wartime, had gained a significant public awareness. All aspects of illumination were subject to drastic reduction ranging through private housing, shops and offices, street lamps, advertising signs and motor vehicles; in fact, any source of lighting that might assist the crews of enemy aircraft to identify their target. In the early hours of 11 August 1939, an opportunity was taken to test vehicles with masked lights under blackout conditions. Between 12.15am and 3.45am, the West End and suburban areas were visited using a new STL whose lights were equipped in accordance with the new regulations. It was found that the interior lighting of the vehicle was quite inadequate for practical purposes, the conductor being unable to see to collect fares and issue tickets. The report also recorded that intending passengers lacked means of identifying buses as no route numbers or destinations were visible and, when boarding and alighting, the platform and stair treads could not be seen.

Appended to the report was a detailed description of the route taken and the hazards encountered, including two near misses with separate cyclists not seen by the bus driver until level with them and failure to see the kerb when stopping, resulting in mounting it on one occasion and coming to rest three feet from it on another. On board the STL were Messrs Wicks and Monson, representing the Board's Technical Officer.

Under the guidance of Frank Pick, the Board's War Emergency Committee had been established in August 1939 to discuss all aspects affecting the Board following the declaration of hostilities. On 6 September, Durrant reported to the Committee upon the position of the 338 chassis currently under construction at AEC's works. Of the order, 150 (programme SY) were more than 20% complete and 188 (programme UB) less than 20% complete. In view of the current circumstances, AEC Chairman C W Reeve had asked for an assessment of the Board's proposals.

Durrant suggested that it might be of advantage to accept delivery of 150 chassis, the ST vehicles they would replace being converted into lorries for Government use, an issue he was requested to pursue with the Ministry of Supply. The War Emergency Committee agreed that Durrant should take up the chassis situation with Reeve to inform him the Board would be prepared to take delivery of all that were in the course of manufacture and to release AEC from completing those not in active production. Once negotiations were complete, the Board's Secretary C G Page would be asked to consider the legal position with regard to AEC's contract. The same day, Durrant sought an interview with AEC's Chairman during which the question of cancellation was discussed. Reeve said that of the RT chassis order, 100 were in the final stages of assembly and could be completed; 50 were in a state of partial construction and could probably be finished without any further action. However, of the remaining 188 chassis, comparatively few parts for their construction were available and special action was considered necessary should AEC succeed in securing the material essential for their completion. Durrant then asked Reeve how the Board would stand if an order for uncompleted chassis was curtailed. Reeve responded by proposing all components would be segregated in a special store at AEC and an inventory prepared. The Board could draw on them as required for which a charge would be raised. However, Reeve reported that supplies of material at Southall were small, a large proportion of the work having been undertaken at the premises of specialist manufacturers. He urged the Board to obtain a priority certificate if the parts were required.

A communication confirming the Board's intention to cancel the order for 188 RT chassis was sent to Reeve by Durrant, his letter also stating that the order for 150 was still required. Reeve replied on 11 September to confirm his acceptance but corrected Durrant's impression that 100 chassis were almost ready for delivery. Instead, 100 sets of parts would reach the final stages of assembly unless AEC was prevented by Government intervention. Regarding the remaining 50, Reeve stated that some could be produced and, if a priority certificate were obtained and instructions given immediately, there was a possibility that all fifty chassis could be built.

The declaration of war was the first item debated by the Joint Experimental Committee when it convened on 7 September 1939. Those in attendance agreed that the future policy of the JEC would be to keep future meetings to a minimum and to limit discussion to those items likely to have a direct bearing on the national economy and any serious defects or questions on the use of alternative materials due to a lack of supplies. Under this remit, the JEC continued to convene alternately at Chiswick and Southall, and despite 2RT chassis production having commenced, many relatively minor modifications in their design were raised for immediate action. Although the order for 188 chassis was formally terminated on 15 September the JEC was not advised until its meeting of 11 October that the Board had issued emergency notice No.133 for the cancellation of programme UB. The committee subsequently agreed that a variation sheet should be appended to London Transport Specification 9638 to confirm this action.

During the meeting of the War Emergency Committee held on 2 October 1939, a report was received from Durrant regarding staff employed in the body building shop at Chiswick Works who would soon be fully employed in the construction of bodies for 2RT chassis. Approximately 75 chassis would be dealt with during the next two months after which no more new bodies would be produced. Durrant reminded the committee that as 150 chassis would be delivered the remainder would be fitted with existing bodies drawn either from vehicles currently in service or from the float of spare bus bodies. The chassis would be sold of any vehicle from which the body was removed for fitting to a 2RT chassis. Pick directed his Chief Engineer to prepare and submit a report that set out his proposals but, with no further action recorded, the plan was subsequently withdrawn.

Durrant provided Frank Pick with an update regarding special expenditure requisition G325 in a memorandum dated 12 October. Of the vehicles approved for construction, 17 STLs had been completed at a cost of £1,621 each. Also recorded in his statement was a reference to the amount of material that had been ordered for use in the manufacture of bodies, but negotiations were in hand with the various traders with the likely result that the Board's commitments would reduce appreciably. The cost of an RT was given as £1,825, this figure comprising £810 for the body and £1,015 for the chassis, the latter amount including a sum of £30 for development costs previously agreed on the assumption that 1,000 RT chassis would be built.

Sinclair went on to report that at a meeting the previous day, officers from the Ministry of Transport, Home Office and Air Ministry had agreed to the use of two headlamps on all public service vehicles if the offside mask were of the new standard Home Office type and that 20W bulbs were used in both headlamps. Durrant reported that to equip all motor buses with the new masks would cost £2,070. He followed this with a message to Pick that read: 'Have ascertained Taw and Co, who supply our headlamps, quote five shillings each for new headlamp masks. Price quoted by another manufacturer in the press was ten shillings per pair. At our works, the cost is estimated at about two shillings each. It therefore appears that manufacturers have a ring agreement, i.e. five shillings each. It is exorbitant and points to a racket'. Authority to use two masked headlamps was received just before the first of the 2RT2 vehicles were completed yet the whole class entered service with only the nearside headlamp in place.

A further requirement of wartime regulations was the application of white paint to the bumpers and running boards of motor cars or equivalent on passenger service vehicles. Arrangements were therefore made for the Board's motorbus fleet to have the forward section of both front wings painted white in addition to the sides and bottom edge of the platform area, the forward pyramid treadplate on each stair and the exterior moulding located at the base of the lowest rear panel to which was also applied a white disc.

According to a document issued by London Transport, the white disc was for the benefit of trolleybus drivers although the purpose of the embellishment is unrecorded. However, from the test of an STL in a simulated blackout, it can be appreciated that driving conditions were extremely hazardous. By identifying the vehicle ahead to be a motor bus, a trolleybus driver would be aware that it could be overtaken without the danger of the poles of his vehicle becoming dewired. He would also be aware that the bus in front might make a turn into a street devoid of overhead wiring.

The wartime lighting restrictions when first applied to road vehicles failed to cover comprehensively regulations for the interior lights other than to state that no light, which was visible from the outside, should be used to illuminate the interior of any vehicle other than a public service vehicle. By the end of December 1939, Chiswick technical staff had produced a document listing the various types of interior lighting cowls to be used on every type of London Transport bus and coach.

The cowls were designed to provide adequate lighting over the seats but would prevent, as far as practicable, rays of light passing through the windows and entrances. The most widely used cowl was conical in shape and on vehicles, such as the RT would be used on the lower deck; the upper deck being provided with a circular cowl with a diameter of approximately 5ins. The cowls were kept in place by a spring wire and the bulbs to be fitted were supplied with a stove enamelled black disc with a diameter of approximately 1¼ins. Appended to the document were sketch plans for each type of vehicle, those for RT 1 and 2RT2 being drawn separately, although the types of cowl fitted to both were identical. Included in the document was a description of the curtain blind installed behind the nearside front window to prevent light from the interior affecting the visibility of the driver. The blind was fitted using an expanding wire, screw eyes and hooks that replicated a domestic method for hanging lightweight curtains. Straps and press-studs were used to secure the blind in opened and closed positions. The blind was stowed against the nearside front corner pillar but due to its suffering from interference by passengers, arrangements were made for it to be stowed against the central bulkhead capping between the two front windows and more easily seen by the conductor.

Possibly taken during the secondment of RT 8 for wartime publicity purposes, this view purports to show a clippie carrying out her duties among a nonchalant group of passengers. The windows have been covered in lightweight material that fails to resemble remotely the netting that will eventually be fitted although the correct style of shade for the interior lights is already in place. Proof that it is not a genuine service photo lies in the fact that tram and trolleybus tickets are being carried.

To provide route number identification during the blackout many of the Board's buses including the RT were fitted with a stencil carrier at the top of the lower deck nearside rearmost window. The area behind the stencil was covered using a white transfer; black paint being applied either side. An experiment with a black/white/ black transfer affixed across the width of the window proved unsuccessful. The interior cowl covering the bulb above the nearside longitudinal seat was especially adapted to light the stencil.

On 8 February, a request was made for a P type pass lamp to be fitted to the offside dumb iron in order to improve the forward lighting of the 2RT2. The Works Engineer at Chiswick was asked to arrange for 150 brackets and necessary wiring to be installed; the lamp was independently switched. In the same month, a further change in lighting was issued which required the fitting of a regulation headlamp mask to all passenger service vehicles by 1 March. The Board currently had two types of lamp in use supplied by CAV Bosch and Taw. Instructions were therefore issued which covered both lamps these specifically relating to the use of a tee square to ensure the lamp was square with the front of the vehicle and a sighting jig so that the beam from the new headlamp mask pointed straight ahead when the vehicle was on level ground.

Perhaps the most bizarre general alteration to restrict the RT's lighting was the use of scrap metal to make a cover for the budget lock key hole in the panel above the rear registration number plate. Presumably, the lighting emitted through the quarter inch square hole was likely to attract the attention of an enemy bomber!

July saw details released of a steering wheel locking device designed to prevent unlawful use of vehicles when left unattended. Two basic types were produced, one secured using a padlock and key, the other with a box spanner, the latter covering most of the Board's bus fleet although there were five design variations, one example especially for the RT.

The Main Technical Committee discussed window protection for buses in late September following Lord Ashfield's request that 80 Country buses and 20 Central area buses be put in service with open lace glued to the glass panes. A permanent wood covering for windows was thought more practical by members of the Committee, because it would be cheaper to replace than lace covered glass. At the time, approximately 400 vehicles had already sustained damage, the windows of some having been boarded up and others covered with Rexine. However, timber was in short supply and the Board's Purchasing Officer was asked to try to secure supplies.

Ashfield's insistence regarding the application of anti-splinter protection to windows did gain support and a number of suggestions were received regarding the type of material that could be applied to the glass. Netting was eventually used with a small area removed through which passengers might peer during the hours of darkness in the hope of finding a landmark. The apertures varied in shape, initially circular, then rectangular but later diamond. However when a shortfall in supplies was experienced an experiment was conducted that substituted reclaimed blind linen for netting, but this material was not found acceptable and would only be reconsidered under very exceptional circumstances. An earlier suggestion for window protection was the use of exposed x-ray film provided by local hospitals, but this was not adopted. An addition to ARP vehicle lighting was issued in a document produced during November 1940, which required the provision of a special cowl for illuminating the platform step and a small area of the roadway or kerb. The unit was rectangular with rounded rear and square front from which light was projected downwards through three vertical slots; it was to be switched on during normal blackout periods.

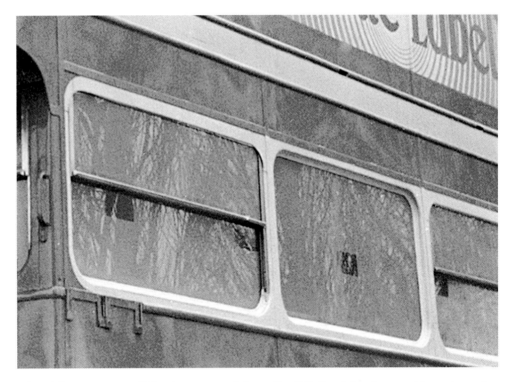

RT 130 has been equipped with anti-blast netting with rectangular vision panels in the material being provided for each seat. This would later be replaced with centrally placed diamond panels on the plain windows only, the half-lights having the netting removed from the upper section.

In July 1941, a modification removed from the RT the driver's nearside rectangular mirror, which was then replaced by a circular one fitted to the corner of the canopy valance. The application of safety netting to the lower deck windows was given as a reason for the removal of the larger mirror although an earlier statement recorded that it might foul the full release of the driver's emergency window.

A general alteration for action at Chiswick and the 2RT2 garages was issued in late September 1941 requiring the removal of the P type lamp from the offside dumb iron and its installation in a new position within the cab dash panel. The lamp remained separately switched.

The Chief Chemist found it necessary to issue a directive in March 1942 regarding the future policy regarding painting now that the availability of paint and its ingredients had decreased by 40% compared with peacetime. He was of the opinion that the period between the painting of RT and STL buses could possibly be extended if the paintwork was good. No doubt Wilford was recalling a situation that had arisen in April 1941 when Ashfield found it necessary to contact T E Thomas, General Manager (Road Transport) after having noticed what he believed to be freshly painted buses on the streets. This, he felt, gave an erroneous impression to the public that the Board was maintaining its vehicles to pre-war standard. Thomas had pointed out that the vehicles were new RT buses entering service, many from store.

Wilford also advocated that the paints difficult to obtain should be substituted by those more abundant. He maintained that supply was vital of the synthetic white paint for application to the rubber wings of buses and that he intended to use a special case prerogative to secure supplies.

Those in attendance at the Chairman's conference at the end of September 1942 would have been given the opportunity to view a bus externally finished to a new standard, the principal colour was oxide red. The committee agreed that oxide red should be used due to a shortage in supply of mail red, the remaining stocks of which would be used to maintain for as long as possible the standard of finish of the Board's railway rolling stock.

Building the 2RT2

During 1939, alterations began at Chiswick works in anticipation of the work involved for the construction of RT bodies. The composite form of body construction adopted for the type required the manufacture of many metal parts and in consequence, the body and metal shops underwent significant changes in layout in order to accommodate the transformation of construction techniques. Chiswick also possessed a considerable stock of seasoned ash, which moved the Chief Stores Superintendent, Percy Croom-Johnson, to draw to Frank Pick's attention, soon after the declaration of hostilities, that the timber had been purchased at pre-war prices and it now formed a valuable asset. He thought that all timber stock should be earmarked for the Board's own use and not for Government work that might be undertaken at the west London works.

In addition to the manufacture of all timber and metal parts specified for the RT2 body, there also existed at Chiswick the facility for producing seat frames, handrails and window pans. However, some of the notable items produced by offsite contractors included the driver's seat, headlamps, half-drop windows, cab emergency exit and front screen.

The London Transport Museum Library has on file a letter from Mr A J Ashdown who was employed at Chiswick as a sheet metal worker. He was promoted in June 1939 to the post of Progress Assistant with responsibility for all metal items produced for the 2RT2. Appended to his letter he detailed the method adopted for the construction of the body and he began by describing the manufacture of the roof, the large panels for which had their seams formed on a long folding machine after which they were joined by hand on a large bench. The whole of the roof would then be shaped to the correct contour on a large panel rolling mill; the front and rear roof domes would be fitted after this stage.

The front bulkhead, behind the cab and engine, was a jig-built, spot-welded assembly constructed in the metal shop. Other components separately manufactured were the lower and upper deck floors, the platform and rear bulkhead, the staircase and cab. Also produced as individual frameworks were the sides for the upper and lower decks, for which the wide bay construction employed flitched pillars spaced at 3ft 11ins intervals.

The complete lower deck floor was fitted to a bogie that in turn was placed on the platform of a lift whose descent was controlled until it reached factory floor level; at this point, the sides of the lower deck, platform and front, and rear bulkheads were fitted. The lift then descended further to allow the upper deck to be assembled and a final lowering saw the complete roof placed into position. The final stage of assembly saw the bogie removed from the lift so that interior and exterior panelling could be undertaken, window pans fitted and glazed and the staircase installed. During the panelling up process, the electrical wiring was installed followed by final finishing that included the fixing of mouldings, handrails and seat frames; the body was then mounted on its chassis and the bus sent for painting.

The livery applied to the 2RT2s, when new, differed from that applied to the prototype. The basic colour was Mail Red, with broken white applied to the centre band and surrounds of the upper and lower deck windows; that encompassing the lower deck windows having radiused corners. The beading separating the upper deck windows from the roof was painted red; this colour also applied to the surround of the front roof box and the rear dome.

By February 1939, consideration was being given to the camouflaging of the roofs of the Board's vehicles, a proposal requiring further input from the Chief Chemist. He estimated that if all bodies were treated as they passed through Chiswick for overhaul, the work would take between 18 and 20 months to complete. This process, carried out at a cost much lower than for the current one coat primer, one coat aluminium system, required the application of only a single colour. Bronze Green was also suggested, this colour then having been adopted by the road transport vehicles belonging to the armed services, but following some deliberation, Wilford upheld his original decision and Transport Grey roofs became standard, including those of the 2RT2s. In October 1941, Wilford reported difficulties might soon be experienced in obtaining stocks of the colour and suggested Anti-Gas Grey paint as a substitute.

The interior of the RT made much use of Rexine-covered cappings around the windows; the upper half was finished in cream, the lower in green with small Rexine covered mouldings over the joins above and below the window with Birmabright polished bracelets to the sides. Antiqued brown Rexine covered the plywood panels below the windows, with linoleum of a lighter shade being affixed to the lower coving panels and front bulkhead. Wooden slatting, once to be found on earlier vehicles covering the whole of the upper and lower deck floors, was used for the central gangways, the upper deck landing and platform; a single wooden strip provided support for the seat frame legs. The area beneath the seats was covered in cork tiling.

The platform commode rail, above the used ticket box, also underwent revision with the lower end being altered to prevent the deposit of mud and dirt and the fitting of splashguards to the rear of all wheel arches was thought essential to reduce mud spatter on the lower body panels. The 2RT2 specification had already called for a long rubber mud flap to be placed at an angle under the platform, as carried on RT 1, its purpose superfluous following attachment of the splashguards; however, no reference is filed regarding its subsequent removal.

Improvement of the driver's visibility had been achieved in a modification to the lower windscreen and as a result, the speedometer unit was repositioned on the cab floor forward of the handbrake steady. This action attracted complaints from drivers, these being passed to Mr J Wicks for investigation although no action appears to have been taken.

A variation in design was authorised during the early weeks of body construction at Chiswick following a request from the Board's drawing office for one new RT2 body to be altered for aesthetic reasons presumably in an attempt to replicate the styling of the prototype. The modification to the front upper deck dome and moulding line was to be carried out under experiment S5489; the extent of the work required was listed as:

1. Existing side window pans to be cut and trimmed
2. Exterior cant rail and waist rail $1^1/_8$ inch aluminium mouldings to be carried up the front corner pillars parallel with contour of window pans
3. Existing front window pans to be altered on outside top and bottom corners
4. Front dome to be extended at each side in a downward direction by the welding of an additional piece
5 The half round aluminium moulding at waist rail under front windows to be superseded by 1x16swg steel joint strip
6 Ash corner blocks to be added to framework
7. The half round aluminium moulding at cant rail above front windows to be extended and carried round parallel with window valence panel at pillars. These mouldings are riveted to the valences. The valences will require alteration to suit new canopy dome shape.

Problems from the Start

A total of 53 new 2RT chassis had been delivered to Chiswick to be fitted with new bodies by the time 1939 drew to a close, the first two examples, being those for RT 15 and RT 23, arriving rather ominously on Friday 13 October. On Tuesday of the following week, the chassis for RT 2 was delivered having been given number O6616750, 661 identifying the unit as an AEC Regent, the prefix O indicating that an oil engine was fitted. A consecutive chassis numbering scheme was employed, the number allocated to RT 2 being the next in sequence to that of the prototype.

In the last days of December, ten complete 2RT2s were taken into stock by London Transport, these being closely followed by a further five on 1 January. By the end of the first week of 1940, all fifteen vehicles had been allocated to Chelverton Road garage to take up the fourteen duties on route 37. It would appear, from photographic evidence, that the spare vehicle occasionally took up a duty on route 22 to which RT 1 had been assigned following its initial allocation to Chelverton Road on 17 July 1939; responsibility for the route transferred to the new Victoria garage on 20 March.

The selection of Chelverton Road as the first garage to receive the RT was first mentioned at a joint meeting of the Board's Operating and Engineering Officers held on 21 June 1939. Such action was partly in response to a request made at a meeting of the Central Bus Committee held on 31 August 1938 that recommended that only one type of bus should work on each route. In support, attention was drawn to the difficulties of operation with mixed types and the effect on conductors working on vehicles with open and closed staircases.

A minor crisis occurred within days of the new buses gaining their PSV licences when many refused to start, or restart despite having been in service for many hours. This situation caused a considerable number of delays most notably when engines failed to fire following involuntary stops in traffic or at the commencement of journeys. In order to counteract such predicaments, drivers were forbidden to stop engines at terminal points or during crew changes. The Main Technical Committee received a report stating that, from the original batch of vehicles delivered to Chelverton Road, only three (RTs 15, 16 and 19) started without difficulty. In an attempt to produce a swift solution, a succession of tests was conducted under experiment S5494, which included a comparison of the starting characteristics of RT 5 from the initial batch with RT 54 then at Hanwell garage awaiting delivery. The test also compared RT 5 and RT 15, of which RT 5 was the poorer starter; yet when the batteries of these vehicles were exchanged RT 15 became the non-starter and RT 5 fired easily. These results supported the theory that a fault existed in either the batteries or the dynamo that maintained their charge.

Although not recorded, it can be safely assumed that the incidence of starting problems delayed further deliveries of 2RT2s. On 13 March 1940, the MTC agreed that, in order to address the situation, the twin 12V 11-plate batteries, originally specified for the vehicles, should be replaced by others containing 19 thin plate groups; eight days were to elapse before Chelverton Road garage received a further batch of new buses so equipped. Later, however, the efficiency of the dynamo would again be brought into question. RT 1 remained unaffected, having been equipped with a battery of different specification as installed in the STLs.

RT 56 entered service from Chelverton Road Garage in the first week of January 1940 during a period that saw the first fifteen vehicles of the type licensed. Taken on 23 March 1940 – the poor film quality disguising its newness – this rare view shows that the modification requested the previous month for the fitting of a P type pass lamp to the offside dumb iron has yet to be completed. The body carried by this vehicle is numbered 290, later fitted to the chassis of RT 85 following its release from Chiswick in March 1947 after a seven-month evaluation period; this body was destroyed when the bus caught fire in service on 21 June 1949.

Far left: RT 42 lays over on the Albert Embankment complete with radiator muff to give extra protection against the winter chill. The bus was allocated to Gillingham Street, Victoria on 1 November 1941 following a fifteen-month absence from service, the last of which was at Nunhead Garage where repairs were made to its air compressor.

Left: Of the fifteen 2RT2s entering service in January 1940, only RTs 15, 16 and 19 were considered good starters, a situation that no doubt influenced the selection of RT 19 as AEC's demonstration vehicle. All photographs of RT 19 with its first body (No. 281) show the vehicle in service with other operators, except this example taken while the vehicle was briefly allocated to Gillingham Street, Victoria Garage from 23 September 1942 to 1 October 1942.

Below: The area above the front upper deck windows of RT 100 was reshaped "for aesthetic reasons" during its construction at Chiswick, which provided the vehicle with a forward upper deck finish reminiscent of RT 1. No opinions were recorded when the experiment closed in September 1941 although the vehicle retained this unique styling until its overhaul in the early months of 1950.

At the end of January 1940, constructional details were submitted to the body shop at Chiswick with a request for the allocation to experiment S5489 of an early body, this being qualified as an example for which the roof had yet to be manufactured. RT 100 became the recipient, the bus entering continuous service from September 1940, its revised styling under scrutiny for the possible production of a more artistically pleasing vehicle. The experiment closed in September 1941 with no results being published. Yet the alterations to the vehicle, that could easily have influenced the design of the post-war variant, were retained until its overhaul in February 1950 when RT 25 received the restyled body in an unrecorded exchange.

Although the fitting of Miller semi-automatic gearboxes to twelve 2RT2s was not taken up, another product of the Self-Changing Gear Trading Company of Coventry was tested under experiment S5718. In April 1939, Ottaway wrote to A Gordon Wilson, a director of the Coventry company, to inform him of the Board's commitment to air operated gearboxes. He therefore invited Gordon Wilson to have examples of 7¾in drum gearboxes converted to air for fitting to a small number of new RTs. The figure to be constructed was settled at six, five to be fitted to buses (RT 147-151), the sixth unit held as a spare. The experiment concluded in 1946, the results for which appear later.

The War Emergency Committee received a further report from Durrant early in 1940 in which he recorded that once delivery of the 150 2RT2 type had concluded, the spare fleet of unlicensed buses suitable for service would number 400. At the time, only one property had been secured for storage, which had originally served as the London Terminal Coach Station although all documentation produced by the Board refers to the premises as 'Red and White Garage' due to ownership having passed to a company of the same name.

The allocation of a further 40 RTs to Chelverton Road on 21 March brought to 55 the number licensed for service, including the prototype and these were allocated to routes 28, 30 and 37, allowing two spares. Bonnet numbers were allocated to 2RT chassis in numerical order although deliveries from AEC to Chiswick did not follow a regular pattern. Bodies were fitted to the first available chassis and as a rule of thumb, the lower the body number, the earlier the bus was licensed.

The 16 buses that had seen the start of RT operation in the capital at the beginning of the year had seen their number reduced by one on 27 January following the selection of RT 19 for demonstration duties. No doubt influencing the choice of this vehicle was its ease of starting, being one of only three not gaining a reputation for failing while in service although the largest but non-standard battery available was fitted during the demonstration period. Experiment S5485 covered the loan to AEC, the Main Technical Committee having been informed of the request on 3 January. At this meeting, Eric Ottaway recommended that with a view to obtaining the best fuel consumption RT 19 should be fitted with a toroidal engine, a 5.2:1 axle ratio and high deflection springs. Although in agreement, Rackham pointed out his intention to fit a 115mm bore engine, this precluding the fitting of the new axle ratio.

It was therefore agreed that Ottaway should settle any changes to the original specification of the vehicle with the AEC Sales Department and subject to the outcome, the following would apply: (a) AEC would be responsible for the mechanical condition of the vehicle both before and after demonstration arranging for the vehicle to be returned to Chiswick as new; (b) the Board to arrange for the repainting of the vehicle and its testing before final release to AEC; and (c) the cost to be charged to AEC. Correspondence held on file shows that Ottaway's modifications were adopted and, thus equipped, RT 19 would tour various operators in the hope of gaining sales. The initiative was in response to the cancellation of the Commercial Vehicle Motor Show that had been scheduled for November 1939, AEC no doubt anxious to address the shortfall in sales that would have been generated by the event.

Ottaway set down his plan for the bus by stating that once repainted, the vehicle would be returned to AEC where it would be equipped with the engine and axle ratio he had proposed. After secondment, RT 19 would be returned to Chiswick where the Experimental team would compare its performance with a standard STL and RT. The largest fuel pump setting possible would be applied that would be consistent with a smoke free exhaust and good fuel consumption. The bus was painted at Chiswick in the light green and cream livery of the Mansfield & District Traction Company, green later replacing the cream initially applied to the roof. Between April 1940 and June 1942 RT 19 is known to have visited 22 undertakings, the vehicle proclaiming itself a 'Regent' RT bus on the forward plain window on both sides of the lower deck.

On Saturday 16 August 1941, RT 19 was returned to Chiswick for bodywork repairs although the damage sustained is not recorded. The following month, Birmingham City Transport submitted a report regarding the demonstration bus, which the Board passed to AEC's Chief Engineer. Mindful of the comments raised from RT 19's visit to Birmingham, the Board decided that a copy of the report and subsequent comments should be filed in the RT Post War Specification File.

A number of adaptations were necessary before RT 19 was loaned to AEC for demonstration purposes, which included the fitting of an engine with toroidal heads. It was also equipped with the largest battery available presumably to ensure that starting up did not became an issue. During the vehicle's tour of approximately 22 operators, some unrecorded damage occurred resulting in the vehicle being returned to Chiswick for repairs.

A matter of concern in the early weeks of the 2RT2s in service affected the intake forward of the front upper deck windows that allowed air to enter through a ventilator incorporated in the inner lining of the front dome. RT 1 had a shutter specified to control the admission of air, operated by the conductor's budget lock key and similar in style to that used on the lower deck of both prototype and production vehicles. Presumably, the need to maintain a constant airflow through the upper deck was considered essential at all times of the year in order to clear tobacco smoke and as a result, the shutters were omitted from the Chiswick built RT2 bodies to calamitous effect. Much to the discomfort of passengers, rainwater and snow entered the upper deck due to the absence of any airflow restriction, which was also given as the cause for front ceiling panels becoming excessively dirty. The response by the Garage Engineer at Chelverton Road was the installation of exterior 'snow baffles' in the gap immediately forward of the front windows, differently shaped panels being required for offside and nearside. However, experiment S5523, initially raised to address the problem, contains a recommendation that an adjustment of the ventilator vanes on the upper deck would alleviate the problem, a suggestion overruled in March 1940 when approval was given for fitting the whole production batch with Chelverton Road-style baffle plates.

During early April the air intake on the top of the engine was found unsatisfactory due to Rexine glued to the cab side panel adjacent to the engine, the same material affecting the efficiency of the compressor anti-freeze intake that was located just above floor level below the driver's seat. The cylinder head cover for all 150 engines was remodelled in order that the air intake could be repositioned at the front and an additional hole was provided through the engine side shield to prevent Rexine from being drawn into the anti-freeze device, which contained a half pint of highly flammable liquid.

Soon after RT 18 entered service, it was selected to be tested under experiment S5495 to consider methods by which engine vibration might be reduced or eliminated, but despite alterations to the flexible mounting of the engine, little was achieved. However, this imperfection was to prove insignificant when compared with the next. The first indication that a serious situation might soon occur came with the issuing on the 10 April of an advice regarding the rotary air compressors fitted to the 2RT chassis. The compressor had been designed to run in tandem with the dynamo from a cardan shaft on the offside of the engine. Correspondence had already taken place with Clayton Dewandre regarding shortcomings of the company's RCGA 7 compressor specified for the air pressure system that operated the brakes, gear change and chassis lubrication facility, but action then taken appears only precautionary. Nevertheless, in early May, an experiment was authorised by the Main Technical Committee and covered the fitting of 'revised material' to the compressors of nine RTs; another experiment raised in early June sought to fit six of the type with an amended design of drive. The Joint Experimental Committee suggested that a compressor manufactured by Westinghouse might replace the RCGA 7 but this was soon discounted due to space limitations and the impracticability of designing, at short notice, a high-speed drive necessary to run the unit.

If May had begun badly for the new vehicles, it was about to worsen following a complaint by the driver of RT 57 that the brakes noticeably faded when the bus was fully laden, this being confirmed by the Board's Operating Section when tests were conducted (experiment S5528). The situation was not related to the recent compressor failures and the problem with RT 57 was soon followed by similar experiences being reported by the drivers of RTs 37, 47 and 73. It was soon discovered that excessive handbrake lever travel occurred when the brake drums were hot and this affected the efficiency of the braking system; the situation was swiftly resolved.

Deliveries at the beginning of June increased to 108 the number of 2RT2s licensed for service; Putney Bridge garage having received its first supply of the type for route 14. The number now available was in excess of the official allocation of 87 vehicles to routes but as the compressors were found to have a service life of just 1,000 miles, many vehicles were now being docked for attention. The official allocation at this time was for 26 on route 14 from Putney Bridge garage, 61 at Chelverton Road for routes 28 (15 buses), 30 (21), 37 (15) and 72 (10).

Despite the efforts of engineering staff, there was limited success in keeping the vehicles operational, which resulted in the withdrawal from service of 20 RTs on 1 July and prompting urgent discussion at Committee level two days later. Here it was reported that a large number of the class was likely to be withdrawn, yet Ottaway was of the opinion that at least 20 should remain in service to monitor various modifications recently carried out or under consideration following earlier experiments. On 31 July, J W Wicks, deputising for Eric Ottaway, informed the Main Technical Committee that, from the following day, in accordance with Ottaway's request, all but 20 of the RTs would be withdrawn from service and that immediate action would be taken to make replacement buses available as soon as possible.

When 20 RTs were taken out of service on 1 July, leaving 88 still licensed, 12 STs from the reserve fleet re-entered service, to be joined by 58 more when a further 68 RTs were withdrawn on 1 August. Throughout the remainder of 1940, 196 STs were relicensed for service, but obviously not all were required to deputise for the absent RTs.

As a result of the significant withdrawal of 2RT2 buses, the Red and White Garage in Clapham, located at 80 Clapham Road South, was used to house 46 RTs – 31 from passenger service and 15 yet to receive their first licence. The former AEC works at Walthamstow stored 33 RTs, of which 22 had been taken out of service and 11 were yet to be licensed. The remainder were dispatched to garages in the Central and Country areas, three being ignominiously requisitioned as guardrooms.

The JEC decided to bring to an end its meetings and that held on 17 June 1940 was to be the last, Rackham stating that his company now needed to concentrate on production for war purposes. A final issue discussed another flaw found in the design of the RT, this originating from the fuel supply feed pump unit. The Board was asked to address the issue and in consequence, experiment S5558 determined the road failures were due to an air-lock in the fuel system, the primary cause being an insufficient filling of the fuel tank.

During September 1940, three RTs were relicensed: RT 39 on the first of the month and RTs 117 and 137 eighteen days later, all having been withdrawn on 1 August. Two new vehicles, RTs 69 and 100, the latter with reshaped front dome, also arrived at Chelverton Road as new vehicles on 19 September but remained unlicensed for two days. This small influx of 2RT2s brought to 25 the number of RTs operating from Chelverton Road, 15 of which were allocated to route 37 and ten to route 72. Adaptations to the air pressure system had been carried out on all 25 2RT2s following various experiments undertaken earlier in the year, but a more decisive strategy was necessary in order to bring about the swift return of the remainder of the delicensed vehicles and those yet to enter service for the first time.

In December, an alteration advice was issued by the Board's Acting Technical Officer which, in order to resolve the current air pressure problems, required the conversion to belt-drive of the existing shaft driven compressor. Initially 50 chassis would be converted involving their original compressors (RCGA 7) being moved within the chassis and connected to the forward gearbox shaft. In early February, it was agreed that advantage should be taken of the delivery of a new type of rotary compressor from Clayton Dewandre, designated RCGA 12. In mid-March 1941 three RTs entered service fitted with the RCGA 12 compressor and at the end of the month 15 RTs had returned to the streets, beginning a trend set to continue until the end of June by which time 80 RTs were in operation. However, correspondence had continued with Clayton Dewandre as it was considered that the installation of the belt-driven RCGA 12 was merely a short-term remedy. A more radical response came in the form of a reciprocating compressor offered by Clayton Dewandre, to which the company had given the reference PCGA 19, with an agreement that twelve vehicles should be selected to receive the new unit from those currently undergoing modification. Although a practical alternative, the PCGA 19 compressor was the only unit available in quantity and considered by some to have a greater capacity than was actually required. No plans exist for the initial installation of belt-driven RCGA 12 rotary compressors, nor was any change in chassis code issued. However, the PCGA 19 needed a saddle slung beneath the chassis frame members with the drive transmitted via V belts and pulleys from the front of the gearbox. As the work involved a change from rotary to reciprocating compressor and an alteration to access the new unit through an additional trap set in the lower deck floor, the chassis received the code 1/2RT and the body RT2/1. The first vehicle converted to the new specification was RT 146, which was then tested under service conditions on routes 65 and 25B during early September.

Following numerous attempts to improve the performance of the compressors, the Main Technical Committee agreed to transfer the drive from the engine to the gearbox and, at the same time, replace the rotary compressor with a reciprocating example. The new configuration is seen here with the compressor mounted on an underslung cradle and driven from an especially fabricated pulley fixed to the forward cardan shaft. The first vehicle converted to the revised arrangement was RT 146 which was successfully road tested on 8 September 1941. In view of alterations being made to both chassis and body, the 50 vehicles eventually converted received the code 1/2RT2/1.

The trials produced appreciable results and RT 146 entered service on 17 September from Putney Bridge garage followed by the conversion and subsequent dispatch of RT 143 to Victoria garage on 1 December. The remaining ten vehicles (RTs 125, 100, 139, 110, 39, 103, 46, 59, 9 and 23) of which seven had been among the 25 retained in service, received gearbox driven reciprocating compressors between September 1941 and March 1943. The results from experiment S5670 recorded that, by June 1945, eleven of the twelve vehicles adapted were still in service, RT 146 having run almost 150,000 miles, but the unit fitted to RT 125 failed after 88,000 miles and was returned to Clayton Dewandre for examination, replacement and comment. Such was the success of the conversion that plans were put in hand for a further 38 buses to be similarly equipped bringing to 50 the number of vehicles with the 1/2RT2/1 classification, the work being undertaken from December 1943 until April 1944. When the conclusion of experiment S5670 was published in June 1945, it contained a recommendation that the remaining one hundred 2RT2s should also be modified.

Another problem emerged during May 1941 following an experiment (S5491) from a year earlier calling for road springs of increased stack height to be fitted to six RTs. Unfortunately, the new springs increased the height of each bus by two inches and in order to avoid fouling the roof of Putney Bridge garage, it became necessary to maintain the RTs at Chelverton Road.

In May 1941, authorisation was given for the chassis of RT 1 to be updated using units standard to the 2RT2. This project was undertaken at Chiswick soon after the proto-type had been released from temporary store at the Red and White Garage. Under the programme, the compressor would have received attention for the return of the vehicle to passenger service, but the approved supplementary work involved the installation of a D 140 gearbox to replace the D 133E that had been originally fitted, a standard fuel tank, and fuel and air pipes of the type fitted to the production vehicles. Additionally, an auxiliary air reservoir was installed to improve gearbox operation. Only in late 1944 was it realised that the chassis frame had been constructed to suit the specially designed prototype body. The Main Technical Committee agreed that, in order to avoid confusion, it was essential that the chassis should only ever be fitted with the original body and consequently would be classified 2/2RT, the complete vehicle receiving the code 2/2RT1. The log card for the vehicle also shows the code of 2/1RT, apparently allocated upon completion of the 1941 revisions.

Keen to discover their condition after operating the RTs under service conditions for a period of two years, the Main Technical Committee authorised experiment S5479 which was completed in June 1942. Three vehicles, RT 7, 9 and 35, were taken to Chiswick where the chassis of each was subjected to thorough examination and, in addition, the body from RT 35 partially dismantled. Each vehicle had been in continuous service, although their engines had recently been exchanged at Chelverton Road garage for overhauled units and in consequence were not inspected. The chassis of all three buses were found in exceptional condition, the body of RT 35, despite a number of minor imperfections easily handled by garage staff, was deemed excellent. In view of the results, it was agreed that the time span between overhauls could be extended to three years, a year longer than the interval for other types. As a result, overhauls of 2RT2s that had completed three years service commenced in 1943. An endorsement of the decision to extend the overhaul period came when RT 125 was selected at random during its first visit to Chiswick for overhaul in June 1943 and a visual inspection conducted of the various components as they were stripped from the chassis.

Due to the tireless efforts of those responsible for its design and the Board's engineering staff the disappointing entry into service of the 2RT2 was eventually turned around as temporary modification was followed by major alteration in an attempt to produce the bus A A M Durrant had planned.

Comparison and Change

Once the RT was fully established at Chelverton Road and Putney Bridge garages, it was inevitable that comparisons would be made between the new bus and its immediate AEC forerunner, the STL; the first documented report appeared in November 1942.

Drivers and conductors who had crewed both types generally preferred the RT but there were points within its design they criticised. For instance, drivers complained that their cab was very cold. As the engine was mounted in a lower position than on the STL, the double shield to the nearside of the cab effectively maintained a lower temperature, a situation apparently exacerbated by a number of holes in the cab floor that created an excessive flow of air. Yet the manual issued for the RT in 1940 claims that a special sealing given to the floor plates rendered the cab draught proof. Another grievance of drivers related to the air supply for the gear change system becoming rapidly exhausted. Sometimes RTs were rendered immobile in the middle of the road following a series of difficult manoeuvres that involved a number of gear changes. A further disadvantage resulted from occasional air compressor failures whereupon all brake and gear change operations were lost.

Conductors' complaints were few, many criticising the handrail positioned below the fare chart, which tended to push them forward on to the platform thereby slowing the process of boarding and alighting. Moreover, the ease of steering associated with the RT allowed drivers to take corners at a greater speed and in consequence, conductors lost their balance.

In commenting upon these problems, S R Geary, Operating Manager (Central Buses), placed on record his thoughts regarding air operation of the gears, the system failing to win his wholehearted support. He stated that drivers suffered no hardship when changing gear on an STL equipped with a fluid flywheel and a Wilson direct selection pre-select gearbox provided this unit was in good condition. He also advocated further work on the development of a full fronted bus, to provide more cab space, lamenting that the Board's only example had been withdrawn. In recording his opinion, Geary failed to recall the conclusions reached by experiment S4099 which looked into the question of improving the appearance of a standard STL with a full fronted driver's cab. The reconstructed vehicle was placed in service prior to the 1935 Commercial Vehicle show and in the report issued in April 1937, the unanimous general opinion found that appearance was the vehicle's only advantage. All round visibility, engine accessibility and noise received a number of negative comments.

Yet Geary still favoured full fronted bus design not only from the point of view of appearance but for the additional accommodation made available for the driver. He denounced Ottaway's opinion that half cab vehicles were better suited to fog by stressing that fewer trolleybuses than motor buses ceased to operate in such conditions. He was also of the opinion that the full front design might offer means of access to the cab from the nearside, although he accepted that no serious difficulties had been encountered with the more conventional offside access. In support of his claim, Geary stated that a cyclist overtaking a stationary bus might be struck by the cab door. He clearly had not thought of the sliding cab door installed on the RT.

Controversially, Geary dismissed the installation of heaters for passengers or drivers but supported any improvement in ventilation and reduction in draught. He became the first person to contest the design of the upper deck front windows, which placed the bar required for their operation directly in the passengers' line of sight. His suggestion that this might be remedied by providing droplights of just four inches on the sides of the upper deck and the removal of any opening mechanism from those installed at the front no doubt influenced a later experiment

Geary thought the staircase designed for the RT reduced an already restricted area by bringing the bottom step closer to the edge of the platform and suggested that the stair-well position on the bus might be recessed by 2–2½ins which would allow the conductor to stand further back. However, this was to be simply achieved by the removal of the grab rail beneath the fare chart, its use deemed unnecessary by passengers and conductors. The covering of the platform floor was also scrutinised by Geary who supported the introduction of serrated rubber, as successfully used on trolleybuses, in place of the traditional oak slats. Wooden slats laid in the gangways resulted in the accumulation of dirt and Geary favoured their replacement but ruled out using linoleum due to its poor wearing qualities that resulted in water accumulation during wet weather. Durrant was later to record that his department had been unable to find a suitable alternative without incurring considerable additional maintenance cost. As an aside, he felt forced to admit that slatted flooring was only one stage beyond the straw covering used in the early horse buses. Nevertheless, the problem remained in finding something that would stand up to constant abrasion from passengers' footwear. Also receiving adverse criticism from Geary was the amount of information displayed by the vehicle with regard to places served and, anticipating the demise of roof boxes, he suggested the route number could be placed adjacent to the final destination. Alternatively, for the benefit of passengers awaiting the arrival of buses, he proposed that the route number displayed at the front could be shown on the nearside corner but none should be shown on the rear as he felt this encouraged buses being boarded after the starting signal had been given.

A more positive report on the 2RT2 was written in March 1943 by W A C Snook, Assistant Chief Engineer at Chiswick, who again compared the new vehicle with the STL listing the principal positive features of the RT as: (a) reduction in driving fatigue; (b) economies in maintenance from the point of view of time, material and labour; (c) improved road performance; (d) strengthened body construction with modified exterior and interior finish giving an improved appearance; (e) extra safety and comfort.

On the subject of engines, Snook reported that the performance achieved from those experimentally fitted with toroidal heads had given excellent results in fuel consumption and service life. Using for comparative purpose the 15STL16 model, Snook noted the similarities between the two types listing two examples: the engine suspension system and the fluid flywheel, judging the performance of the latter as being in need of improvement. Front and rear axles on the RT and STL were similar but the brake drums on the RT were of an improved design, resulting in cooler running brakes and tyres and an extension in the life of these components. The characteristics of the road springs were identical but where the RT had the edge over the STL was in its steering and controls for which considerably less effort was required in their operation. This distinct advantage was enhanced by the introduction of an improved driving position made possible by a lower radiator position and a larger cab window.

Drivers' visibility later became the subject of experiment S6138 following a warning by Durrant that authorities might in future frame the regulations governing vehicle construction to encompass this characteristic. Tests were conducted using bus types 15STL, 2RT and 2G and three trolleybuses. Results were obtained by plotting at ground level the limits of vision of a driver of normal height, comfortably seated and, from the bus types under inspection, the RT was by far the best.

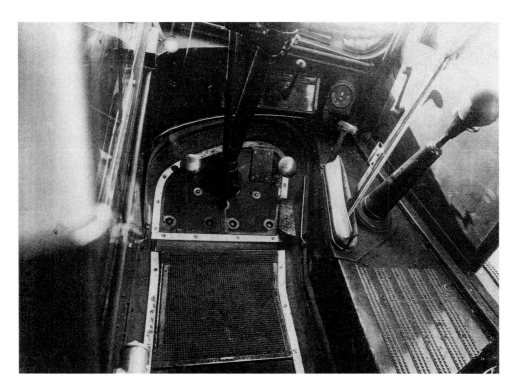

The inherent structural weaknesses of the STL body had been met by using more metal in the RT's build, its design aiming to eliminate the ingress of water suffered by earlier bodies that led to rotting of body pillars. The RT staircase was more robust than the STL's and added to the general strength of the structure. For the passenger, droplights were made for ease of operation, although problems had arisen soon after the 2RT2 was introduced and the manufacturer, Hallam, Sleigh, and Cheston was asked to effect modifications to the gearing. Snook was also of the opinion that the external contour of the RT was more pleasing to the eye.

The garage-docking period for the RT had been extended to 20,000 miles, which occurred after approximately six months in service; the STL was docked after completing 12,000 miles. This gave the number of man hours spent on the RT per annum as 290, the STL requiring 359. Finally, the RT's air powered chassis lubrication system was held partly responsible for the extension of the vehicle's overhaul period from two to three years.

Within three months of his report, Snook took part in discussions with the Board's accountant and Chief Financial Officer regarding maintenance costs of the STL and RT types. It was immediately recognised that direct comparison would be misleading due to the average age of the vehicles concerned, that for the RT being three years, for the STL, seven. In addition, there had been many improvisations introduced into maintenance practice enforced by a shortage of material in the case of the STL, while maintenance of the RT was substantially in accordance with normal pre-war practices due to the availability of spare parts.

Experiment S5468, authorised on 8 November 1939, involved the fitting of toroidal cylinder heads and pistons to six RT engines (recoded A185A); the vehicles initially involved being RTs 4, 10, 39, 44, 59 and 68, all initially allocated to Chelverton Road garage. Foremost in the minds of the Joint Experimental Committee members was the fuel efficiency of the vehicles so equipped. Of the six converted, three had been provided with a rear axle with a ratio of 5.2:1.

It was not until mid-December 1943 that a six-week test could be conducted. By then, all vehicles fitted with toroidal engines had been allocated to Putney Bridge garage where they could be matched with RTs powered by pot cavity engines on a heavy traffic route through central London for which route 14 was admirably suited. The vehicles involved in the testing were RTs 2, 19, 39, 68, 70 and 108, some engine exchanges having taken place with the first vehicles fitted with the A185A. RTs 111, 146 and 147 with pot combustion chamber engines were used for comparison. The five buses with toroidal cylinder heads achieved 9.1mpg during the experiment and the pot cavity ones 8.22mpg. Unfortunately, vehicles with 5.2:1 axle ratios (RTs 4, 39 and 44) could not be incorporated in the foregoing data, two due to the earlier failure of their toroidal engines, which had necessitated the installation of pot combustion replacements. RT 39's results were therefore discounted, the vehicle being the only example fitted with a toroidal engine and 5.2:1 axle ratio.

By the end of October 1944, the actual number of toroidal engines installed in 2RT2s was causing confusion, prompting a Chiswick employee to record that a total of seven were now in existence, the additional unit having been fitted to RT 19 during its tour as a demonstration vehicle. He then reported that two engines were still fitted to RT 39 and RT 70 and that three had been found in the Engine Detail Section leaving two engines to be traced. In the absence of further documentation, their fate is not known. The conclusion of experiment S5468 requested that toroidal direct injection engines should be fitted to all future RT chassis and consideration be given to converting all existing engines with pot cavity cylinder heads to toroidal. In addition, further tests with 5.2:1 differential gears were recommended and in consequence, rear axle differential ratios became the subject of experiment S5992 opened in February 1945 to determine whether changing the ratio from 5.75:1 to 5.2:1 would improve axle durability and fuel consumption. Arrangements were made to record and compare four standard with four experimental vehicles, the results showing an increase in differential life. An average of the fuel consumption for the four vehicles fitted with 5.2:1 differentials (RTs 6,43,55,79) produced a figure 11.15 gallons per hundred miles, that for the standard vehicles (RTs 7,23,30,40) was 10.98. Experiment S5970 was issued on 21 December 1944 under which 25 RTs would be fitted with toroidal engines, but this was abandoned on 17 April 1946, with no further conversions having taken place. Instead it was agreed that the whole fleet of 150 vehicles would be converted. This work was also never undertaken and a new toroidal engine (A204) was subsequently selected for the post-war RT.

The log cards for RT 147 to RT 151 record the five vehicles as having been fitted with Coventry gearboxes, the description relating to another product of the Midlands-based Self Changing Gear Company. Six examples of the Wilson 7¾in gearbox were manufactured under licence for air pressure operation by the Board whose policy regarding such development had remained unsettled until April 1939. Initially experiment S5335 and later experiment S5718 were allocated for service experience with this type of box to be obtained, each having a smaller diameter running gear than the D140 units currently fitted to the rest of the class.

The boxes remained under scrutiny throughout the war and considerable problems were experienced due to maintenance difficulties brought about by design weaknesses and a lack of spare parts; most being non-standard. All six gearboxes were used; the number fitted to each vehicle being RT 147 (2), RT 148 (3), RT 149 (4), RT 150 (3) and RT 151 (3). Apart from their unreliability, the units were incapable of being used to drive the compressor as used for the 50 1/2RT chassis conversions. On 6 September 1946, a decision was made to replace all 7¾in gearboxes with standard units.

Experiment S5965 was raised in May 1944 to look into the installation of leather and Vynide (leathercloth) seat coverings that had been fitted to two STLs and four RTs. Three of the RTs operating from Putney Bridge had their seats trimmed throughout

either in leather (RT 74), Vynide (RT 78) or a combination of both (RT 76), while RT 128 at Chelverton Road had a part installation using both materials; all entering service so equipped between August and October 1944. While the experiment was in progress, Vynide became the standard material used in the trimming of the Board's buses. The material gave excellent service for 3 to 3½ years but, when it became more readily available, the material of choice was moquette.

During April 1945, RT 98 was loaned to AEC for the purpose of suspension tests. The vehicle underwent adaptation in order that it could be tested in the measurement of "roll". Once the results were to hand, they were to be used in formulating the standard of the maximum acceptable limit for the company's work in the development of suspension. If any of the modifications by AEC remained after the tests, they may have influenced the selection of RT 98, many years later, as the skid bus used at the Chiswick driver training school.

Perhaps the most obvious change to the outward appearance of six members of the 2RT2 fleet occurred between September 1947 and January 1949 following the fitting of new windows manufactured by Hallam, Sleigh and Cheston. Curiously described as 'half-drop with high guard rail', the windows on the sides of the vehicles could be opened approximately a quarter of the glazed area, those at the front on both decks for a shorter distance. All new windows were fitted during overhaul, under experiment S5158 authorised by the Main Technical Committee on 1 May 1946; the vehicles involved are listed in the adjacent table.

Four of the buses with the new windows were officially inspected on 21 July 1950 at Putney Bridge garage and it was found that the windows appeared to be standing up to service conditions, although frequent breakages had occurred, the glass in the moving section having not been provided

Stock No.	Date Fitted
RT 82	7 February 1949
RT 84	5 July 1948
RT 101	21 November 1947
RT 121	12 September 1947
RT 127	20 December 1947
RT 129	13 April 1948

Six 2RT2s were fitted with specially designed opening windows in order to address the control of air entering the RT and the criticism regarding the position of the centre bar on half-drop windows. Although the modification was deemed too late to be incorporated in the design of the 3RT3, the RF single deck and Routemaster buses were so equipped.

with a protective channel on the lower edge. Some adjustment had been necessary to allow the guardrail with its winding mechanism to be cleaned as previously this component appeared dirty when viewed from the outside of the vehicle. Nevertheless, the advantages of the windows were: (1) The guardrail was clear of the average passenger's eye line; this addressed a number of complaints received regarding the design of the 2RT2 windows upon their entry into service; (2) Any draught from the windows was kept above passengers' heads; (3) The weight of the moving section of window was considerably lighter and consequently reduced the wear on the operating mechanism. The recommendation of the experiment was that all future double deck vehicles should be designed with similar opening windows although their retrospective introduction for the existing fleet was not an economic proposition. The RF class was so equipped as indeed was the Routemaster.

Some vehicles continued to be selected for further experiments such as S6359, which was given the title 'Semi-Enclosed Air Pressure System'. The buses involved were RTs 2, 6, 7, 8, 39 and 111, each being fitted with a large metal box placed inside the cab. The box contained 15lbs of silica gel, used to dry completely the air passing through it; this replaced the compressor anti-freeze device. Experiments of a similar nature have not been included in this book but S6359 has special significance. Although the experiment closed in July 1951 after some four years of testing, the equipment remained in situ as can be exemplified by RT 8. When the vehicle was repatriated for restoration by the Ensignbus Company in 2005 after some 44 years in the St Louis Transport Museum in the USA, it was found to have the silica gel box still fitted in the cab. In addition RT8's offside dumb iron plate, which might be expected to read 1/2RT2/1, has been replaced with another bearing the classification 2/2RT1/2 presumably to identify the bus as part of experiment S6359. Neither the Main Technical Committee minutes nor the surviving documentation covering the experiment mention a change in classification.

Experiment S6062 was authorised by the MTC on 14 November 1945 and required a 2RT2 to be fitted with a new style of driver's seat manufactured by Hallam, Sleigh and Cheston and known as the Widney Patent 'Farno'. The seat obviously proved successful, being fitted to 65 4STD3 and 21 1TD1 buses. However, RT 113 remained the only 2RT2 to receive the new seat; it was subsequently removed.

Planning for Peace

In the spring of 1941, the Board's bus rolling stock requirements after the war were discussed in memoranda between Engineer-in-Chief V A M Robertson and the Chairman's Secretary, B H Harbour. Robertson's main concern was the age of the current fleet. He considered that although buses achieving 15 years in service must be declared obsolete, every attempt should be made to reach that maximum in full safety if spare parts were readily available although this action was only deemed economic under the current emergency. Nevertheless, he suggested that the purchase of new vehicles remained a viable alternative to the repair of older ones. He therefore recommended that the peacetime life span for double deck vehicles should be 12 years and ten and eight years for large and small single deck types. Any replacement programme, however, would have to allow for the limit of 527 bodies per annum, which, under the LPTB Act of 1933, the Board was permitted to build in its own works. Any beyond this quantity would need to be purchased from outside manufacturers at prices higher than the in-house cost. Of timely consideration was the prospect for rebuilding the County and City of London following the recent period of intense bombing administered by Hitler's Luftwaffe which gave little chance for an assessment of future operating requirements. In addition, further vehicles would undoubtedly require replacement, their loss anticipated as a direct result of the war.

In order to make further progress, a Post War Planning Committee was established in December 1942, under the chairmanship of Harbour, to consider all aspects of the Board's operations in the aftermath of the current conflict. The Committee was required to report on the operating considerations and requirements that would have to be taken into account in the construction, design and equipment of the post-war standard types of buses, coaches and trolleybuses.

Pre-empting the remit of the Committee, M J H Bruce, Works Engineer (Chiswick) produced a report entitled 'Considerations Affecting the Post War Bus Replacement Programme'. Writing in July 1942, Bruce recorded that of great importance were the general characteristics of passenger carrying vehicles within the fleet and the selection of actual types needed to achieve maintenance requirements and alteration due to changes in legal restrictions. Accordingly, with the assistance of S R Geary, Operations Manager (Central Buses) and A H Hawkins, General Manager (Country Buses and Coaches), Bruce set down his plan for the composition of the post-war fleet comprising five categories of buses as follows:

Category	Description	Remarks
I	General purpose double deck bus	For either coach or bus operation, according to body fitted
II	General purpose 2-man single deck bus	As above
III	General purpose 1-man single deck bus	For feeder services
Ia	Special purpose (low height) double deck bus	For low bridge routes
IIa	Special purpose 2-man single deck bus	For low and weak bridge routes

Hawkins was of the opinion that the employment of double deck coaches should be extended to the maximum limit and in consequence recorded that the vehicle, which responded to the requirements of category I, was destined to become the mainstay of the new Green Line fleet.

Before the war, the phasing in of replacement vehicles had been on an irregular basis and had caused any possible standardisation to deteriorate rapidly, resulting in an excessive number of differing types. This situation failed to reflect the economic maintenance strategy that had last existed in 1928 when the fleet consisted of three principal types, a large number of the parts of two being interchangeable. But in 1942, there existed 14 basic types of chassis and 12 types of body and within both groups, numerous variations were also to be found. A return to the standardisation of component parts was therefore set down as essential. This, together with a rigorous control over the range of future chassis and bodies would result in a policy of economic operation and maintenance. In conflict with such a measure was the need for the Board to take advantage of progress being made in design and manufacturing techniques. However, by the adoption of a planned policy of periodical phases in design for development and testing in service, there existed a possibility for taking, at successive intervals, early advantage of an initiative that would succeed in the retention of a limited variety of bodies and chassis within the current composition of the fleet.

The problem of swift obsolescence remained a significant feature of the Board's thinking, and, in order to address the situation, it was proposed that regular changes in the basic design of vehicles should take place every six years. If adopted, the scheme would result in three basic types of vehicle in service for five years out of every six. At the same time, opportunity would be taken to vary and improve upon the colour scheme and saloon interiors every sixth year during the extensive refurbishment of each bus that was expected to occur at this time in its life. By implementing a reasonable degree of standardisation to suit the maintenance and building programme, a level of diversity would exist that would preserve the Board's policy for a high standard of comfort coupled with the most recent advances in design.

Fluctuations in the rate of vehicle replacement in the period 1929–1939 had resulted in some disturbance in building programmes at Chiswick Works and at other manufacturers supplying buses for the Board. To avoid a repetition, the post-war building programme would be planned to match the maximum rate by which the large number of obsolete types could be replaced without seriously influencing the corresponding programme for the next replacement cycle.

By 1942, the practice at Chiswick was to conduct a full overhaul of each bus at two-yearly intervals, the figure having been gradually attained since 1930 when the previous criterion of annual overhauls was in place; the reduction in frequency had been made possible by improvements in the durability of new designs. A greater gap between overhauls was thought possible following the introduction of all-metal bodies and an increase to three years had already been recommended for the 2RT2s following the thorough examination of the body from RT 35 earlier in the year. A final visit to the works would take place two years before the end of service life adopted for each bus. The planned first replacement cycle would produce the need for 800 new vehicles during each of the first three years necessitating the building of approximately 300 bodies per annum by outside contractors after which body construction would be undertaken using the Board's own facilities at Chiswick. The figure of 800 new vehicles per annum had been calculated to reduce, with minimum delay, the large number of ST and LT types built in 1930–1932, of which 2,224 remained in service and were soon to exceed their functional life span. Moreover, by the fourth year of post-war replacement, all buses dating from 1933 or earlier would have been displaced.

Some serious deliberation had been given to the type of post-war chassis to be selected which remained dependent on the possibility of confining immediate post-war purchases of chassis to AEC – a course of action endorsed by W A Snook (Acting Chief Engineer Buses and Coaches), A A M Durrant and E C Ottaway. All were of the opinion that experience had shown satisfactory and economic service could be best obtained by using vehicles built to the Board's own specification based upon results in service. The Board's senior officers had stressed a need for economies in maintenance and in consequence, the adoption of the RT as the basic type was set to lead the standardisation of the fleet. A complete specification and detailed drawings of the vehicle could be made available for competitive tender. The suggestion that the post-war fleet should consist of five basic types gave rise to the notion that the RT chassis could undergo frame modification and used for all principal types with the exception of the single-deck one-man operated bus, resulting in the fleet comprising only two principal types of chassis. Those responsible for the design of the RT body agreed that there existed no reason for any departure from its system of construction.

In considering the limitations applied to vehicle construction, the thorny question of weight restriction had been recently revised. At the start of the war, regulations required a loading of 7.5 tons per axle for double deck vehicles with a maximum laden weight of eleven tons; further discussions with the Ministry were likely to see this lifted to eight tons, although the initial objective had been nine. This restriction passed to the designer the distribution of unladen weight whereupon additional latitude was available when assessing the weight of chassis components. In the event of a concession being granted, some alterations in design were considered likely. Yet the advantage of an extended life made possible by the use of more robust components had to be measured against increased running costs that would arise from an additional unproductive weight; nevertheless, the net result was deemed beneficial.

The dimensions of passenger service vehicles were the subject of similar discussion, the objective being to secure sanction for a vehicle of up to 30ft in length and up to 8ft in width. In 1942, the maximum capacity required of a double deck bus was 60 passengers although this was only in demand during the morning and afternoon peak hours, during each of which buses could usually achieve one return journey. Nevertheless, some thoughts were also being voiced regarding the introduction of a 48-seat bus with provision for 20 standing passengers. The RT's seating capacity was considered satisfactory and other changes in its design recommended by the operating departments were of minor character with one exception. This involved the fitting of doors to double deck buses for country operation and double deck coaches for use when required, but the former category had attracted adverse comment. Among the minor changes in the design of the RT came a request for a lower-deck cord-operated bell and a distinct sound warning for the driver (e.g. a buzzer) from the upper deck. The return to a cord-operated bell was considered by some a retrograde step but owed its suggestion to the neat appearance in London trolleybuses. More positively, the amount of electric cabling and maintenance was reduced due to fewer bell pushes of which the 2RT2 had two in the lower deck ceiling panels; the two bell pushes located in the platform area were to be retained.

The general appearance of the 2RT2 then came in for scrutiny, some criticism having been levelled at its design, which appeared top heavy to some. This was considered to have arisen from the colour distribution and three variations of livery were produced for consideration. In the face of some opposition to the need for separate roof route number boxes, an opinion had already been voiced in support of their retention by T E Thomas, then General Manager (Road Transport). To many officers there was little doubt that the adoption of a red colour mass above the intermediate floor level of double deck buses made for a heavier looking vehicle especially when the travelling public had, in past years, become used to lighter treatments in this area.

A series of paintings were found while research for this book was being undertaken, presumably produced in order that officers might select a style of livery for the RT. One example is marked "existing scheme but without roof service numbers (roof boxes)" which is almost correct although the roof should be grey. A second variation brings down the silver of the roof to cover the rear dome while a third makes use of the between decks band to create a black stripe above an enlarged white window area in trying to emulate STL livery.

NEAR SIDE

FRONT   REAR

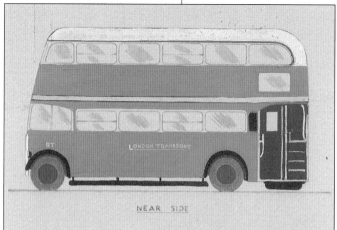

NEAR SIDE

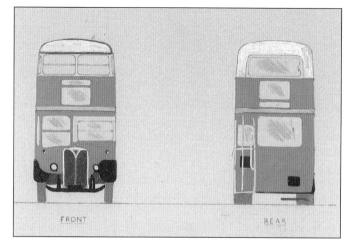

FRONT   REAR

NEAR SIDE

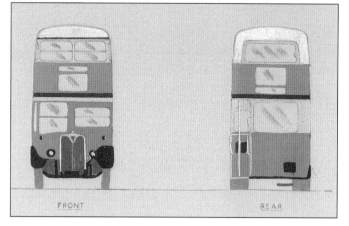

FRONT   REAR

The person responsible for the commissioning of the paintings no doubt saw fit to have photographs produced showing RT 1 without its front and rear roof boxes. This manipulation makes little sense, as the blind display has no provision for a route number.

Despite being considered a key issue, the establishing of a uniform bus-building programme for a minimum variety of types still extracted a comment that any new design introduced would not be entirely free from subsequent alteration. A study conducted on the subject of the costly alterations to types entering service during the past fourteen years brought into sharp focus the need for adequate prior development.

Notwithstanding the RT's four year development programme, a call was made for a period during which would be collated all evidence available in order to prepare designs and rectify prototypes. And on the subject of experimentation, a request was made for an operating fleet of up to fifty vehicles to be sanctioned comprising examples of the various types purchased to date or especially built. These vehicles would be placed in revenue service but would be maintained under the direct control of the Technical Officer and would constitute a development fleet envisaged as the basis of trials the results of which becoming the source of debate for future designs.

Worthy of note was Bruce's final statement in which he declared that although the Board was known to have many outside imitators, it lacked competitors in its own particular field. In avoiding any temptation to take advantage of this position, the Board could refrain from too frequent changes in its equipment, echoing the earlier sentiments of Lord Ashfield. Yet such a notion was opposed by V A M Robertson, who recorded that there remained much to learn from others and emphasised the need to maintain contact with operators particularly those adjacent to the LPTB area. Robertson stated that comfort and appearance remained essential requirements and should these parameters, when adopted by other companies, be better than the Board had, a move should be made to adapt their methods and design.

The recommendations contained in Bruce's report can be summarised as follows:

1. A basic life of twelve years should be adopted for all vehicles.
2. The type of chassis for most vehicles should be the RT for the first six years of replacement. The chassis should include such modifications as could be developed by the end of the war.
3. The basic type of body for double-deck vehicles should be the RT as currently designed and that a suitable single deck body should be developed upon the same lines as soon as circumstances permitted.
4. Every step should be taken to finalise decisions regarding weight and width restrictions.
5. Changes involving basic design of chassis and body should be arranged at intervals of six years; development occurring in the intervals with a view to finalising designs to be successively adopted as standard.
6. A development fleet to be sanctioned to form part of the operating fleet, which would be under the observation and control of the Technical Officer, decisions regarding future types being based on the observed performance and experience gained from using such a fleet.
7. A lighter colour scheme to be adopted for Central buses above the intermediate floor and that roof route number boxes be abolished in the future to avoid a top-heavy appearance.

In September, Bruce replied to Robertson who had criticised a number of issues in the report. In response to the Engineer-in-Chief's suggestion that the war might have some influence on the development of engines, Bruce further supported his proposal for the establishing of a development fleet that could offer scope for testing. Undoubtedly, discussion regarding the design of post-war buses continued after the publication of Bruce's report but little was committed to paper.

It was acknowledged that the limitations imposed by the regulations governing vehicle size had severely hampered the design of road passenger vehicles. Many organisations, including the Board, were currently preparing a memorandum for submission to the Minister of War Transport seeking some moderation in the dimensions applied to passenger service vehicles that would allow designs to meet the future demands of bus travel in London. The principal changes being sought were: (1) The elimination of the third axle for vehicles built to the maximum permissible overall length of 30ft; (2) The maximum permissible width for all public services vehicles to be 8ft; (3) The maximum permissible unladen weight of a public service vehicle to be 9½ tons with no restriction placed on the maximum vehicle weight. Considerable discussion on the issue of vehicle width had taken place and many comments made such as those in Bruce's earlier report. The maximum width of 8ft was now permitted in most countries outside Great Britain, a fact of which most correspondents were aware. Adding some strength to the request was the insufficient room provided for two passengers of average size occupying the same transverse seat on buses of 7ft 6in width. This effectively reduced the distance across the gangway and hindered conductors from efficiently carrying out their duties, especially when standing passengers were also being carried.

The report then reviewed some aspects of bus design; the first being the position of entrances and exits. It was acknowledged that, for the majority of the Board's double deck fleet, the conventional rear platform continued to be favoured. The complete opposite was to be found in the USA where the latest double deck designs for New York and Chicago placed the entrance forward of the front wheels. A forward entrance design for some STL double-deck buses had been adopted by the Board in 1934/1935 to address complaints frequently made by Country area passengers that the open platform at the rear allowed dust, mud and fumes to be drawn into the bus by the vacuum created during deceleration.

The original batch of 12 forward entrance STLs had been equipped with a door across the entrance, this being subsequently omitted from the order for 133 that followed which were fitted instead with a specially fabricated wind shield. This patented shield was designed to eliminate draughts and rain from entering the vehicle but the arrangement proved unsatisfactory and was the source of constant passenger complaint. The General Manager of Country Buses and Coaches, A H Hawkins, had therefore recommended that all front entrance vehicles should be fitted with a door. From the information gathered by the Committee, the current rationale that determined the siting of entrances should ignore the reasoning behind the decision to build the front entrance vehicles in 1934/35, as the difficulty could have been avoided by the provision of a door to enclose the rear platform. At the time, the advantages for front entrance buses were:

(a) improvements to the external design of the vehicle could be made;
(b) passengers could not attempt to board or alight whilst the vehicle was in motion so much as they could on rear entrance types;
(c) improvements in fare collection efficiency. Conductors in the Country area had found an advantage in collecting fares by approaching passengers from the front, many of whom would have their fare ready;
(d) the front platform allowed a greater supervision of passengers by the conductor who would be in a position to detect over-riding more readily;
(e) the driver had a better view of boarding and alighting operations.

Morden station on 20 May 1944 finds RT 38 on route 93. Although the vehicle was among the first few to enter service in January 1940, it was withdrawn the following July and sent for storage to the London Terminal Coach Station in Clapham Road. Once work to improve its failing compressor was completed, it returned to the streets in April 1941 spending the majority of its war years at Gillingham Street and Putney Bridge garages.

In taking the design a stage further, the Committee also considered modern American practice for single deck buses that provided a separate entrance and exit thereby reducing delays by two opposing streams of passengers using a single entrance/exit. The report deduced that although no rationale existed for double deck vehicles to be similarly constructed, there would be too great a sacrifice of seating on the lower deck to support the recommendation. The Committee also declared that a separate entrance and exit arrangement only appeared feasible within a flat fare system, which allowed the conductor time to supervise passengers alighting and boarding, no thought having yet been given to a pay-as-you-board arrangement. Having considered each of the points relating to centre entrances and vehicles with forward entrances, immediately behind the front wheels, the report concluded that from an operating point of view, the conventional rear entrance still had the advantage.

Moving to passenger carrying capacity, the Committee noted in its report that, due to wartime conditions, a greater number of standing passengers had been permitted, but such dispensation was unlikely to be continued indefinitely following a return to peacetime conditions. Nevertheless, for new vehicles, revision of the regulations to provide adequate space for additional standing room could not be ruled out. As previously recorded, when the question of vehicle width was under consideration, the existing standard designs, including the RT, did not make proper provision for standing passengers who tended to congregate between the longitudinal seats on the lower deck where the gangway was wider. The Committee's view was that standing accommodation should be strictly limited, as experience had shown that, even for the shortest journeys, the average bus passenger preferred a seat.

The report assumed that should larger capacity vehicles be introduced on practically every route then a decrease in mileage during peak hours would result. In consequence, a reduction in the number of vehicles employed during peak periods would permit a reduced difference between peak and normal services, a factor that would lead to an economy in mileage and the avoidance of waste in the use of manpower. A larger vehicle would also permit a reduction in mileage during off peak times on routes where headways could be increased without depressing the traffic. Such an eventuality was considered likely in the initial post-war period following restrictions in the use of rubber and fuel oil, when larger capacity vehicles would be required to carry the anticipated volume of traffic. A different viewpoint was offered by A H Hawkins who doubted whether a double deck vehicle of larger capacity could be economically employed in the Country area, where no significant disparity existed between normal and peak hour services.

Ottaway recalled that 30ft long buses had been a subject for discussion by another panel set up by the Board, which reached the conclusion that the greater road space required when turning would preclude the operation of longer buses on certain routes in London. A similar problem had been envisaged when vehicles of 8ft width were considered. He also added that the Operating Department had expressed a preference for buses with 56 seats not only from the aspect of licensing duty, which was based on passenger capacity, but also in the maximum number of those seated at any one time whose fares could be easily collected. In confirming that there existed no engineering reason to preclude the construction of a motor bus of similar dimensions to a trolleybus, Ottaway stated that, until the Ministry changed the regulations, a vehicle with three axles would be required. Also in need of consideration was the wear imposed on the rear tyres of vehicles with three axles, which was far in excess of those with two, due to the continual 'scrubbing' action that occurred when turning. Nevertheless, he stated that the 2RT engine (A185) had been designed with future development in mind and could be suitably modified to power a larger vehicle.

RT3 Production – Chassis

The first meeting of the Joint Consultative Committee was held at Southall on 5 October 1944 with G J Rackham and Colonel Trench representing AEC and Eric Ottaway the LPTB, all of whom agreed that, when conditions improved, testing procedures would resume for the assessment of proposed post-war improvements to the bus fleet. The first new development project requested by the Committee was the conversion of an existing 2RT chassis to incorporate principal amendments arising from wartime operation. Rackham was awaiting authority from the Board of Trade for his company to manufacture a limited number of post-war vehicles for experimental purposes and forewarned his committee colleagues that unless an early decision came on post-war regulations governing construction, the development of the post-war chassis would be seriously delayed and their early delivery jeopardised. It was now possible for AEC to continue with the design of the RT chassis incorporating the joint experience of the company and the Board; however, work could not proceed until the principal dimensions had been established. Ottaway responded by requesting a swift preparation of the post-war 3RT chassis layout to enable the completion of an assessment of body dimensions and interchangeabilty. Rackham then advised the Committee that AEC had decided to introduce the RT as a standard type thereby making it available to other operators. Yet in so doing, AEC made a number of variations to the design from which it became clear that London Transport was not departing from the AEC standard but AEC was departing from the standard specified by London Transport. This would eventually lead to some provincial operators expressing disappointment that certain features of the AEC Regent MkIII were different from the Board's 3RT model.

Earlier in the year, A B B Valentine, the Chief Supplies Officer had entered into negotiations with AEC for a renewal of the company's contract with the Board. A S C Chattey, AEC's General Sales Manager, had requested a proviso whereby supply should be limited to not more than 600 chassis or 20% of the company's output in any year, whichever was the greater but Valentine thought it not unreasonable to request 750 chassis or 25% of the company's annual output. During the second meeting of the JCC held on 21 December 1944, Rackham announced that AEC had been authorised by the Board of Trade to recommence production of civilian vehicles and in consequence, the company anticipated production of the Board's standard RT chassis by December 1945. In consequence, he believed that within a short period of time, production for the Board could be built up to a rate of 10 per week and predicted further increases of up to 20% of AEC's total production during 1946.

Rackham also stated that the terms of release by the Board of Trade were subject to the chassis being ordered directly by the Board but negotiations were yet to be conducted with the Ministry of War Transport regarding the allocation of quantities. The MOWT had recently rejected proposed alterations to vehicle dimensions and mindful of this decision, the JCC agreed to recommend that the Board should order 500 RT chassis from AEC to the approved post-war specification for delivery commencing December 1945, increasing to a rate of ten per week as quickly as possible. In view of the decision made by the MOWT, the bodies and chassis would be constructed under the prevailing regulations and, in general, to the latest RT design. Further developments in chassis production could be introduced after completion of the first batch of 500 vehicles, which represented approximately one-year's production. The same principle applied to body manufacture, which might undergo revision should the current restriction on maximum width be relaxed from 7ft 6ins to 8ft.

Rackham then sought authority to cancel the manufacture of an experimental RT body since the alterations now contemplated for the first batch were not of sufficient magnitude to warrant its construction. In consequence, he requested that the chassis from RT 52 currently on loan to AEC, which had been equipped with a selection of post-war improvements, be rapidly fitted with an RT2 body to allow the assessment of service experience. The JCC allocated experiment S5972 to the project.

RT 52 was among the second batch of 38 vehicles whose chassis were converted to 1/2RT configuration, the work being undertaken during its first overhaul that concluded on 20 April 1944. Two months later, on 18 June 1944, RT 87 was damaged in a V1 incident and after recovery was taken to Chiswick. RT 52 is recorded as being at Chiswick on 22 June its body (No. 299) being fitted to RT 87 which re-entered service just over one week later. At the same time, the damaged body from RT 87 was mounted, although not fitted, to RT 52 only to be removed four days later when the chassis was sent to Southall. The action of placing a damaged body on a recently overhauled chassis is questionable although, in documentation later issued regarding the experiment, RT 52 is recorded as having been damaged by enemy action and its body scrapped; neither detail is accurate.

One of the more significant alterations required for the 2RT chassis was the fitting of a toroidal engine with uprated rear flexible suspension. Also to be installed were a modified fuel pump, a new design of fluid flywheel, improved controls for the selector gear within the gearbox and a more reliable starter motor. Further improvements would be made to the handbrake and the mushroom head of the gear change pedal was to be altered to match the oblong shape of the footbrake. The gearbox would now provide the drive for the compressor and dynamo, following the specification originally proposed for the chassis in 1937.

During the final months of the war, the Joint Experimental Committee requested that RT 52 be sent to Southall in order that it could be converted to match the specification developed for the 3RT. When AEC returned the chassis, it was fitted with some – but certainly not all – of the proposed adaptations including a toroidal engine and this supposedly improved layout for driving both the dynamo and compressor from the gearbox, both units being mounted on the offside of the chassis.

Electrical failures had continued to concentrate the minds of the Board's Main Technical Committee members who were of the opinion that the dynamo drive system was the most likely cause. Originally sharing the same engine-driven jackshaft as the compressor, the dynamo was found to be inadequately charging the batteries, a conclusion reached some years earlier when poor starting of the vehicles was under investigation. Of some concern to the MTC was the life of the 2RT2 dynamo, which was given as only 62,000 miles when compared to a similar installation on the LT type that lasted 186,000 miles. Fifteen RTs (including RT 8 and RT 113) had their dynamo drives modified to one of three different arrangements most of which failed, none being recommended for adoption.

In the outcome, the chassis of RT 52 did not receive every planned modification. From the original list of changes, only the toroidal engine and fuel pump were fitted, the fly-wheel was altered but not replaced and the handbrake improved. In addition, further work extended the revisions made the previous April and the dynamo became a gearbox driven unit in addition to the compressor, both being positioned on the offside of the frame. The JCC subsequently requested that another chassis be loaned to AEC in order that it could be converted as the prototype production RT incorporating all improvements now planned for the type and upon its return, a standard body was to be fitted for service operation. Included with the paperwork for experiment S5972 is a document seeking an allocation for the cost to produce one post-war RT platform mock-up that was presumably required in order that an RT2 body might be adapted for mounting on a tail-less chassis specified for the 3RT3. In the outcome, no reduction was made to the length of RT 52's chassis, such curtailing being reserved for the next chassis supplied for conversion.

On 27 March 1945, AEC returned the chassis from RT 52 to Chiswick where await-ing its arrival was the overhauled body removed from RT 19, whose chassis was then despatched to Southall. Once the floor traps had been modified to provide simpler access to the repositioned units, RT 52 entered service trials at Putney Bridge garage on 4 May where, two weeks later, the engine was found to be vibrating considerably and became very erratic when idling. After corrections, no further faults are filed for RT 52, whose experimental status was withdrawn in January 1946 in view of the imminent return of RT 19 under experiment S6026. Upon arrival at Southall, RT 19's chassis was soon referred to as the 3RT3 prototype.

With the return of RT 52 from AEC came another request for a 2RT chassis to be converted to 3RT configuration. The Board sent the chassis from RT 19 to Southall but decided to match its development by undertaking the conversion of another chassis and selected that from RT 46. The chassis was retained at Chiswick, being equipped with a resited dynamo on the nearside of the frame opposite the retained rotary compressor in anticipation of the conversion of the remaining 100 2RT chassis to approximate the post-war specification. Despite this preparatory work, RT46 never officially received the later specification of 3/2RT2/2 and eventually returned to service as one of the 50 earlier modifications of which it had been part.

When the JCC convened on 9 February 1945, the specification for the 3RT3 was approved, only to be altered at the next meeting in June following changes made during the conversion of the chassis of RT 19 to represent the post-war prototype. One of the most noticeable revisions was the fitting of a battery cradle beneath the staircase suitable for four AEC standard 6-volt batteries, access to which would be gained by means of a detachable panel in the side of the body. When in need of replacement, the twin 12-volt batteries supplied for the RT2 chassis required manhandling across the platform. During the course of conversion, several units were removed from RT 19's chassis and, with the exception of the engine, these were returned to Chiswick for development work under experiment S6017.

At the JCC meeting held at Southall on 3 July 1945, following Ottaway's lead, the members agreed that they should receive and consider all points relative to the design, new production procedure, material and experiments in connection with new chassis programmes for London Transport. G J Rackham then advised the members of the Committee that as soon as design control was abolished, AEC would introduce a revised suspension system, larger tyres and other improvements for the Regent Mk III chassis that it would then offer for sale to provincial operators. Ottaway thereupon requested an analysis of costs be prepared that compared the Board's chassis with those produced for other concerns.

RT 19's chassis was scheduled for delivery to Chiswick on 27 July 1945 although the vehicle's log card records this event as having taken place on 3 August. Surprisingly, it was returned with the dynamo driven directly from the engine instead of the gearbox as specified for the post-war vehicles, no doubt causing the interim chassis code of 2/2RT to be issued. In October 1946, during another visit to AEC, the post-war arrangement was installed and the chassis coded 3RT. For its delivery to Chiswick, a structure for the driver had been fixed to the chassis and this was retained to facilitate its delivery for inspection by Park Royal Coachworks and Weymann Motor Bodies. The structure would also be used to transfer the chassis to Maidstone & District Motor Services for the company's appraisal.

Due to the tail-less feature of the post-war chassis, RT3 bodies would be strengthened accordingly. Apart from RT 19, the only example of a similar design was the chassis built for RT 1 and in view of the delay in designing and manufacturing an RT3 body, it was arranged for that from RT 1 to be fitted to the prototype 3RT chassis. This is recorded to have taken place on 27 November 1945 and the resulting vehicle numbered RT 19, its seating capacity being increased from 55 to 56 on 25 February following a relaxation in the regulations regarding the unladen weight of vehicles. Although the Board intended conducting a series of road tests before RT 19 re-entered service, the Experimental Section was unable to retain the vehicle for sufficient length of time to allow these to be undertaken. This was due to the need to carry out tilt tests and review fuel and oil consumption under service conditions.

The body from RT 1 underwent a number of changes on pairing with the 3RT proto-type chassis in order to replicate the design envisaged for RT3 bodies. Some alterations were purely cosmetic for the purpose of inspection while others were permanent such as the deletion of the offside platform window, still present despite a request made in 1938 for its removal before construction of the 2RT2s commenced. The insertion of a plain panel to the rear of the lower deck windows on the offside ensured that the route stencil holder was also lost.

However, one series of tests at this time in which RT 19 did become involved was experiment S6118 entitled 'Acceleration Tests: Trolleybuses and RT Buses'; the other participant was F1 class trolleybus 743. For the experiment, a level stretch of roadway was selected between the Hampton Court entrance to Bushy Park and Kingston Bridge where the traffic was slight and did not interfere with the test. The results were derived from an average of at least six runs in each direction which effectively minimised the effect of variations due to wind speed and road gradient. The data consisted of the times taken to accelerate from rest to maximum speed, the result in seconds being recorded against the appropriate intermediate speeds. Two main series of tests were conducted, the same recording apparatus being used for both vehicles. The tests with RT 19 were undertaken with two fuel pump settings in consideration of the fact that, when the new RTs first appeared on the streets their engine power would be restricted due to the many older vehicles with smaller engine capacity remaining in service alongside them on the same routes. However, there was some anticipation a higher setting might be adopted for the RT engine and tests with the fuel pump so adjusted were completed in order to indicate the true performance of the RT.

The first road tests took place on Tuesday 5 February 1946 for which trolleybus 743 was supplied with a crew of seven in addition to the driver; RT 19 carried the equivalent of 56 passengers in addition to its two-man crew. Three sets of results were produced from the data obtained comprising a single entry for trolleybus 743 and two for RT 19, its fuel pump having been adjusted accordingly. Two days later, similar trials took place but on this occasion, 743 carried the equivalent of 70 passengers and a two-man crew and RT 19, a driver and a crew of 5. In their unloaded conditions, RT 19 reached 35mph in 33.7 seconds with its fuel pump at a lower setting and 23 seconds when adjusted for high power; 743 took 26.1 seconds. When fully loaded, RT 19 reached 30mph at 33.7 and 24 seconds while the trolleybus took 33.8 seconds. However, in both sets of tests, 743 reached a speed of 20mph faster than RT 19 despite the bus being modified for optimum operation.

RT 19 was not relicensed for service until 25 February 1946 when it was dispatched to Chelverton Road, being transferred four days later to Putney Bridge for a seven-month period in passenger service. Code 3RT3 was initially allocated but then 3RT1 in order to identify the vehicle as having been fitted with the prototype body.

It would appear that the Board decided to undertake its own conversion and selected RT 46 when the vehicle arrived for overhaul at Chiswick on 3 June 1946. Experiment S6152 was allocated to the project the object of which was the installation of a revised system for driving the dynamo and compressor assimilating as closely as possible the arrangement previously established for the 3RT3.

The adaptations at Chiswick saw the earlier modification removed and a new reciprocating compressor and dynamo relocated respectively on the offside and nearside of the chassis frame. In these positions, if the tension of the driving belts remained relatively equal, the stresses they placed on the mainshaft of the gearbox were reduced. Due to the design of the 3RT chassis being narrower than the 2RT's it was not possible to use the drive belts and pulleys specified for the post-war model. Some smaller changes were undertaken involving a change of fuel pipes and adoption of the 3RT handbrake gear.

After conversion, on 9 July 1946, RT 46 received Body No. 318 from RT 23, which was removed and replaced on 21 August by Body No. 338 from RT 94; two days later, the bus was sent to Putney Bridge garage. On 26 August, Chiswick requested the return of the vehicle, the body requiring traps to be cut into the floor to facilitate servicing of the repositioned units. The bus was later inspected by members of the Development Section but retained at Chiswick until early November 1946 when it was returned to Putney Bridge. The log card for RT 46 shows the issue of three separate chassis codes, 1/2RT, 2/2RT and 3/2RT, causing a clerk to request for his records, clarification of the correct code upon the vehicle's next overhaul.

Although the experiment for which RT 46 was selected is entitled 'Conversion of RT Chassis to RT3 Prototype', RT 19 remains the only vehicle identified with this work. Nevertheless, among the extensive documentation produced describing the adaptations to RT 46 is a statement that the work was done before authorisation was given for similar conversions of the 100 2RT2s yet to be modified.

Right: Only RTs 7, 19 and 39 received the interim post-war livery that called for the beading around the top deck windows to be painted cream to match the central band. Soon after the prototype body was mounted on the chassis from RT 19, following its conversion to 3RT configuration, a series of tilt tests was conducted to ensure the stipulated minimum angle of 28 degrees was achieved. This proved a difficult task during the first tests conducted in early 1946 but with some alterations to both bus and tilting machine, the required angle was achieved on 19 March.

On 21 January 1946, RT 19 underwent a series of tilt tests conducted jointly by AEC and the Board to ascertain the practicability of the chassis being fitted with an 8ft wide body when restrictions were withdrawn. Under experiment S6141, the results were initially compared with those of a Mansfield & District Regent Mk II, the testing team indicating that some difficulty might be encountered in reaching the statutory angle with the 3RT and that this would be worse with an 8ft wide body. When the Mansfield & District bus was fitted with London Transport road springs, it attained a tilting angle of 29 degrees, the statutory requirement being 28 degrees, which RT 19 eventually achieved after changes to its suspension and the tilting machine had been overhauled. This result was again attained after RT 19 had both axles extended to assimilate conditions applicable to an 8ft wide vehicle. However, despite further tests, the examiners concluded it impracticable to calculate the estimated increase in the centre of gravity and its effect on the tilting angle for the proposed 8ft vehicle until a body of that dimension was fitted.

Members of the JEC again convened on 20 February 1946 to be advised that the Ministry of Transport had sanctioned the use of 8ft vehicles on certain routes. During the discussion that followed, the Committee agreed to consider the effect of this decision on the present 3RT chassis programme and schemes were soon evolved for utilising the increase in vehicle width. These mainly concerned possible adaptation of the chassis frame and the fitting of larger wheels and tyres. However, any such variations would require the Board's approval, whose design team would be asked to provide AEC with data relative to the estimated weight of a wider body by demonstrating the stability of such vehicles following a concern that the width concession might affect the legal requirements for tilting. In addition, the tyre track would be broadened but in consideration of the point at which mud splashing on the body would occur. At the same meeting, it was announced that an 8ft-wide mock up body had been built at Chiswick. A second series of tilt tests took place on 29 March 1946 with another, but this time unrecorded, Regent Mk II being used for comparison, the results showing that the centre of gravity on the RT was higher. Suggestions for improvement were made by members of the JCC and further tests were requested once the best combination of springs and axle frame straps had been determined. The committee also noted that the Regent Mk II was fitted with an AEC torsion bar, in effect a metal bar that acted as a spring with one end secured to the chassis frame and the other to the axle. The committee requested AEC design a torsion bar with suitable road springs for the 3RT suspension system and subsequently increase its angle of tilt. Recent trends in the design of bus chassis had resulted in a reduction in the pitch of road springs and consequently a deterioration of tilting angle and, to improve vehicle stability, the JCC recommended that the width of the chassis frame for the 8ft wide bus be increased accordingly.

Chiswick took delivery of the first 3RT chassis (O961031 for RT 152) at the end of March 1946, the JCC being advised of this significant event at its mid-April meeting. When the chassis was placed on the weighbridge, its total weight without fuel, water or batteries was 1cwt 3qr 5lb (91kg) above the weight of the prototype chassis; no satisfactory reason could be given for the increase. Two experiment numbers were allocated to the testing of the wider vehicle. S6167 under the title 'Route Certification Vehicle' quotes the chassis from RT 155 and RT 169 as having been fitted with mock-up 8ft bodies built at Chiswick. Conversely, S6162 entitled '8ft Wide Bus' refers instead to two chassis being used for the same purpose: O961023 delivered on 15 May followed by O961037 on 28 May; modifications to each were effected by the fitment of special studs that allowed the wheels to be set away from the hubs. The compiler of the first experiment report quoted the bonnet numbers initially allocated; upon return to service O961037 and O961023 became RT 2436 and RT 1117.

An inspector employed by the Board was based at Southall to oversee chassis assembly. In applying to each chassis the principle of rigid interchangeabilty, it was evident that all controlling dimensions had to fall within fixed tolerances. All parties agreed that, where quantity production was involved, it was difficult and impracticable to assess accurately all relevant dimensions using standard equipment. A special gauge was therefore designed and manufactured, to be lowered on to the chassis using a special sling, allowing all major points of construction to be swiftly examined. Among the main areas checked were the body mounting points and the position of the radiator, to ensure correct clearances around the cab. Also inspected were the correct fitting of the bonnet and the alignment of the rear axle to confirm the overall width of the vehicle and ensure correct clearance within the wheel arches. Completed chassis were initially delivered to MAP (Ministry of Aircraft Production), store 877, Aldenham Railway Depot, Elstree, but once production was under way new chassis were also sent directly to other storage sites at Reigate garage and Slough at the former bus garage in Langley Road. Soon completed chassis were being delivered to Weymann and Park Royal directly from AEC at Southall.

On 20 June 1946, the JCC discussed the specification for the second batch of 500 Regent Mk III vehicles. With production of the first batch underway, the Committee became acutely aware that the only means of ensuring the new buses would pass the tilt test was by the fitting of a torsion bar to the rear axle and special damper plates to the front springs. As RT 19 had been so modified, the committee agreed that road tests should be conducted to determine the effect on the vehicle's rolling characteristics. At the same meeting, the AEC representative stated that if the chassis frame width was to be increased for the 8ft wide vehicle, then production by the company could not be entertained before 1948. If the standard but modified frame were retained, then supplies could commence in about September 1947. Ottaway thought that the Board's position regarding the development of an 8ft wide bus must be assessed in consideration of demand for such vehicles and the current commitment to those of 7ft 6in width. In addition, he urged that the most suitable type of 8ft chassis be obtained and standardised. The JCC sought swift action that would allow headway for chassis and body design to be established in advance of production and requested Ottaway contact AEC's Sales Manager with an outline of the Board's requirements. However, the Committee noted that should a chassis of increased frame width be produced, it would be necessary to build and mount a prototype body for tilt testing before AEC committed to production.

By July, the draft specification for the second order of 3RT chassis was submitted to the JCC and approved for circulation. The committee was asked to consider all 500 vehicles being built to the narrower specification and its members subsequently decided to adhere to the current 3RT width of 7ft 6ins unless alteration was requested by higher authority. Also of interest to the JCC was the near-completion of the prototype mono-bloc engine at Southall, which Ottaway had agreed to test plus two additional examples in 3RT chassis with a view to subsequent adoption. RT 19 was initially identified as being the recipient of the first engine but delays resulted in the prototype engine being fitted instead to RT 179 for testing at Leyton garage from mid-September 1947. It was soon removed due to unacceptable mechanical noise and replaced by a standard A204 engine.

Special torsion bars and damper plates incorporated into the suspension system for RT 19 allowed the bus to pass the tilt test and observations made during its service trials indicated that control exerted by the torsion bars during cornering was easily discernible. In addition, a slight pitching was evident at the front of the vehicle. RT 19 was then returned to AEC for a production model torsion bar to be fitted to the vehicle before it re-entered revenue service. The JCC remained perplexed that the centre of gravity for RT 19 was eight inches higher when compared with the Regent Mk II and every effort was made to lower this figure. As a rule of thumb, a reduction of four inches in the centre of gravity provided a one-degree improvement in the angle of tilt. It was now evident that the production 3RT chassis required similar amendment and it was agreed that all new units, currently stored at Aldenham, should be modified by London Transport engineers.

Durrant had previously recorded that Leyland Motors Ltd was the only manufacturer in a position to supply chassis to a standard comparable to the RT, incorporating features found necessary for operation in London. An initial approach was made to Leyland during the summer of 1946 regarding the construction of chassis, 1,000 of which would be to the Board's requirements and incorporated a marked degree of interchangeabilty with the AEC RT, deliveries of which could commence at the end of 1947 and spread over a period of 2½ years. Durrant had also received confirmation from Leyland that the whole order could be changed to an 8ft specification subject to notification being sent by December 1946 or during the delivery period by giving three months' notice.

At the meeting of the JCC held in July, Ottaway confirmed that authorisation was being sought for the operation of 8ft wide buses but until a sufficient number of routes had been identified, a minimum order of 500 chassis would be held in abeyance. He also confirmed that AEC would be advised of an impending order to allow the company

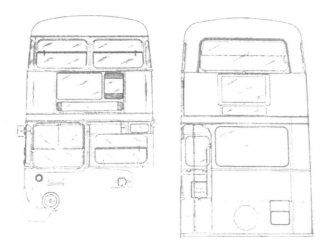

The plan for the 8ft wide RT4 was drawn when bodies of such dimension were to be fitted to chassis of both Leyland and AEC manufacture. However, it soon became clear that AEC could not supply chassis as swiftly as first intimated and the whole project was taken up with Leyland whereupon a contract was issued for a large experimental batch of 500 vehicles.

sufficient time to set up production. The Board subsequently agreed with its existing suppliers that the tooling and equipment necessary for the 8ft vehicle should be manufactured as soon as the design work had been completed and stocks of parts placed in store that were particular to the wider bus. This would enable suppliers to change over to the 8ft design after receiving three months' notice with a result that deliveries could commence after June 1947.

Problems arose in July when the Board's inspector at Southall reported that AEC was experiencing difficulty in checking the agreed modifications to the chassis already completed for delivery. 56 variations had been approved by the JCC since the first plans had been produced and almost half had not been circulated, the situation causing AEC some difficulty in identifying unmodified chassis. The JCC placed the ball firmly in the Board's court and requested that contact be made with AEC's Works Manager.

August 1946 saw the specification for the second order of 3RT chassis once more under discussion. The revised specification would now apply to 250 7ft 6in wide chassis with arrangements made for 250 further sets of chassis components to be produced, common to 7ft 6in and 8ft wide chassis. It is unclear whether Leyland was to have a hand in the construction of the 250 chassis built for both vehicle types. However, during the previous month reference was made to AEC's collaboration with Leyland regarding advice in the manufacture of pre-selective gearboxes for chassis to be built by the Lancashire company. This arrangement was later extended to cover the supply of parts such as the fluid flywheel, which did not feature in Leyland products, the company preferring to market its manual synchromesh gear changing system.

Writing to the Board's Chairman on 24 September 1946, Durrant placed on record that some consideration had been given to the development of a chassisless bus with the intention that this new design might be available for production at the conclusion of the RT programme in 1950. The specification of the four-wheel vehicle would include substantial improvements in springing, engine mounting and general passenger amenities. Durrant estimated that £2,500 would be required to undertake development work before proceeding to the design and construction of a prototype. Experimental work connected with the project would include the fitting of doors and heating equipment on standard RT vehicles that were to be operated as coaches at the end of 1947 followed by the preparation of designs for an entirely new type of double deck coach for production in 1949. The RTs used temporarily as coaches would be of a type that could be suitable for subsequent use as Country buses when the new luxury coach became available. This is probably the earliest reference to the development of the Routemaster, the luxury coach mentioned being RTC 1.

In November, some concern was raised about the overall height of the 3RT3, the torsion bar and road springs resulting in a rear overall height of 14ft 4$^{13}/_{16}$ in. Ottaway stated that the absolute maximum he was prepared to accept was 14ft 4in due to the restricted entrances to some of the Board's garages and he requested immediate changes to the suspension system. In January 1947, Ottaway informed the JCC that the second order for 500 chassis would be for 7ft 6in vehicles only as the first order for 8ft chassis would now be entirely built by Leyland. However, in order that the vehicle body would remain standard and interchangeable on chassis built by Leyland and AEC, it would be necessary for AEC to arrange the springing of its chassis to maintain a height limit of 14ft 4in, although this might be relaxed upon completion of the forthcoming garage improvement programme.

It was not until July 1947 that the JCC was informed that the Board had completed negotiations with Leyland Motors regarding the supply of 8ft chassis. The chassis were to be considered a large experimental batch to allow the relevant authorities to examine the general position regarding their use. Leyland had designed a chassis to meet the Board's specific requirements from engineering and operating points of view and in consequence, the Board was designing an 8ft wide body based on dimensions supplied by the company. The AEC representative informed those present at the meeting that he did not feel the moment opportune to deliberate upon standardisation of 8ft chassis dimensions but stated that the matter could be reconsidered in January 1948 when the Leyland design was more advanced. He regretted that AEC could no longer adhere to the previous agreement to supply 8ft chassis within three months of receiving instructions from the Board.

On 11 July 1946, RT 85 was received at Chiswick for its second overhaul, but within a few days, its chassis had been selected for experiment S6156. This was an examination to determine the extent of wear exhibited by a 2RT chassis following six years' operation under wartime maintenance procedures. On 25 July, a demonstration was arranged for the Main Technical Committee during which the previously removed main components were displayed and the condition of each noted which, in a number of cases, was extremely poor.

The overhauled body from RT 85 was fitted to RT 43 on 1 August and on the same date, RT 85's chassis was officially withdrawn, eventually remaining at Chiswick for some seven months. In a memorandum dated 27 August, J W Wicks, Assistant Engineer (Development, Buses and Coaches) reported that he understood the chassis frame was required to replace that of a service bus, which had cracked. In consequence, the previously removed components from RT 85 would be held at Chiswick until a new chassis could be erected. No further details remain regarding this initiative and the log card for RT 85 states that the vehicle re-entered service on 19 March 1947 having been fitted with the Body from RT 56. The bus was destroyed by fire on 14 May 1949, reducing the number of 2RT2s in stock from 150 to 149.

In early 1947, members of the Board's Main Technical Committee considered the alterations made to RT 46. They agreed that when the conversion took place of the remaining 100 vehicles to the revised specification, the code 3/2RT2/2 would be allocated. The new reciprocating compressor fitted would be that designed for the 3RT; but the existing dynamo would be reinstalled. In a footnote to a list of cancelled work previously approved by the MTC dated 6 May 1949, Eric Ottaway requested that further consideration should be given to the value of converting 100 vehicles to 3/2RT2/2 specification when measured against the material supply position. He stated that a costly conversion programme would be necessary and in support recorded that most 2RT2 buses had now received their last heavy overhaul. A work programme to uprate the remaining 99 unconverted 2RT2 buses was eventually approved, the number being reduced by one due to the earlier destruction by fire of RT 85. RT 52, whose chassis had been the subject of earlier adaptations, was also converted bringing the total to 100.

RT3 Production – Bodies

The London Aircraft Production Group had been formed in April 1940 comprising Park Royal Coachworks, Chrysler Motors of Kew, Express Motors and Body Works of Enfield and Duple Motor Bodies of Hendon whose manufacturing capabilities were overseen by the Board that in turn gave overall control to Eric Ottaway. As a result, 710 four-engined Handley Page Halifax bombers were constructed for the RAF. Each of the contributing companies undertook the manufacture of a specific section of the aircraft, the technique requiring total accuracy in order to achieve utmost precision during final assembly, which was undertaken by the Board at Leavesden airfield north west of Watford. To achieve such a principle, the Group used a process known as "photo lofting" which had been developed by the Handley Page Company and used in the construction of its aircraft. This required each component to be drawn full size, the resulting master plans being photographed on to the designated material for full-scale layout reproduction; a process that could be continually repeated with the risk of error eliminated. Thus, the previous difficult and often lengthy methods employed in the transfer of designs to metal or other materials were entirely avoided.

In pursuit of complete standardisation, the Board adopted the photo lofting technique for the RT body with the master plans for construction jigs and tools produced in the Chiswick drawing office. However, having had first hand experience in the management of a specialised construction group, Ottaway had no doubt given considerable thought to the mass production of standardised bodies after the war. In a paper written in early February 1945, Ottaway proposed that a company be formed to undertake the manufacture of the Board's requirements for bus bodies and associated spare parts. The capital would be subscribed in equal shares by Park Royal Coachworks, Duple and Metropolitan-Cammell-Weymann. Ottaway's proposal was based upon a general understanding that the Board's requirements for bus bodies related to a fleet of approximately 6,000 vehicles with an average replacement of 13½ years but with a higher rate of replacement in the immediate post-war period to allow arrears to be recovered. He also suggested that the minimum number of bodies built per annum be guaranteed. Despite gaining some support Ottaway's plan was rejected.

The Board's Comptroller, L C Hawkins, submitted a memorandum to the Board in early April in which he outlined the costs of purchasing 500 RTs. Estimated as £1,625,000, the figure comprised £750,000 for the purchase of 500 chassis from AEC at £1,500 each and £875,000 for the purchase from an outside contractor of 500 RT bodies at £1,750. The assumed total cost of £3,250 for each 3RT3 when compared with the average cost for each 2RT2 at £2,023 gave an increase of 60.6% (much of which would have been due to wartime inflation).

The 500 new vehicles were to be treated as 'Renewals in Advance', the initial proposal of utilising them to displace 500 LT and ST petrol-engined vehicles being deferred, when some doubt was raised regarding an early scrapping of the older vehicles. Under prevailing regulations, the new vehicles could only be financed from the trust fund set up for arrears of maintenance under the Railway Control Agreement, the provisions of which allowed a sum equivalent to the current replacement cost of displaced vehicles on a like-for-like basis. The value placed on the 500 older vehicles was £551,000 and in consequence, the Board was required to meet the balance from its own resources but with no additional funds available, the Board was obliged to borrow the amount from the trust fund.

As previously recorded, the 1933 Act that brought about the creation of the LPTB contained a statutory limitation by which the number of bodies built by the Board should not exceed 527 per annum. Up to the conclusion of the RT2 body construction programme, such provision was considered sufficient to cover most of the Board's requirements. However, following the cessation of hostilities, A B Valentine, Chief Supplies Officer, stated that the Board would require new buses at a rate of 750 per year for several years in order to overtake gradually the significant shortfall of replacement. At the same time, the heavy arrears of maintenance would absorb the whole of the available capacity at Chiswick works and arrangements would have to be made for the Board to purchase substantial quantities of new bodies from outside companies for at least five or six years.

Since an early stage of the war, the Ministry of War Transport in conjunction with the Ministry of Supply had controlled both the allocation and, indirectly, the price of both chassis and bodies. Early in the summer of 1945, at the request of both ministries, the main allocation of buses to the Board was to consist of chassis built by AEC and bodies built by Park Royal Coachworks Ltd and Weymann's Ltd in approximately equal proportions. Although the cost for bodies would be the subject of negotiation, that for chassis supplied by AEC would be in accordance with the agreement signed the previous year. Valentine confidently predicted that the demand for new bus bodies was likely to exceed supply for about three or four years or possibly longer. In consequence, he thought it not only advisable to secure the most favourable prices for bodies to be allocated by the Ministry during 1946 but also for subsequent requirements, which, he conjectured, would not be subjected to any controls and could be purchased by the Board from other companies. Identical draft agreements, with changes made where necessary, were therefore signed with Metropolitan-Cammell-Weymann Motor Bodies Ltd and Park Royal Coachworks Ltd for the supply of bodies for five years from 1 October 1945 to 30 September 1950, subject to the approval of the Board and the Minister of War Transport. Metropolitan-Cammell-Weymann (MCW) had been established in 1932 to market the products of Weymann and Metropolitan Cammell, both companies having begun building bus bodies in 1929. Later, the Board placed on record that, as Metropolitan-Cammell-Weymann Motor Bodies Ltd was in technical association with Weymann Motor Bodies Ltd, MCW could take full advantage of the production experience of its sister company in the manufacture of bus bodies. The termination date for both agreements coincided with the expiry of the AEC contract for the supply of chassis and spare parts, with a result that the Board had the fullest freedom, when the time came, to review its future policy regarding the purchase of new buses. In addition, the manufacturers would have the maximum incentive during the currency of the agreements to satisfy the Board in respect of quality and price in order to encourage the Board to offer them new contracts following the anticipated reduction in demand after 1950, rather than resume manufacture at Chiswick.

The agreements with Weymann and Park Royal specified a minimum number of bodies to be purchased each year and a maximum should the Board so require. The maximum in both agreements was expressed as a specific figure or 25% of each firm's total output of bodies, whichever was the greater, there being some uncertainty regarding the total output from the two companies while the agreements were in force. However, in the table below, the third column represents the estimated maximum number of bodies the Board would be entitled to acquire on the basis of 25% of total output at least in the final two or three years of the agreements.

Park Royal Coachworks Ltd	250 min	350 max	500 (25%)
Weymann's Ltd	200 min	250 max	300 (25%)

Valentine considered it impracticable for either manufacturer to supply the minimum number of bodies during the period ending 30 September 1946, as production was not scheduled to commence until early that year. The rationale behind his thinking centred on a gradual increase in production as labour and materials became available. In addition, the Board was unlikely to require as many bodies in the first year since deliveries of chassis might fall short of requirements.

Contained within the existing design control was a directive that made AEC responsible for the provision of the driver's cab to London Transport's drawings. In order to reduce anticipated delays due to AEC having to work with the coachbuilders, Rackham agreed to advise Weymann's and Park Royal to accept the Board's drawings and technical direction regarding the manufacture of cabs. This was later changed after the JCC agreed that the drawings and relevant cab details should be supplied to AEC in order that the company could place orders directly with both bodybuilders.

In early May 1946, Park Royal delivered to Chiswick under experiment S6163 a sample bay section of an RT3 lower deck to demonstrate the construction method and interior finish. The bay section was placed in the laboratory where it underwent specific tests such as the effect of the ceiling colour on interior illumination. In October 1946, newly incorporated company Park Royal Vehicles Limited acquired the whole of the issued share capital of Park Royal Coachworks Ltd. The old company continued trading until 31 December when the the new company took over its assets and undertaking.

Despite having been debated at some length in his previous submission, M J H Bruce's concerns about the livery for the post-war fleet continued to be a topic for discussion. In July 1945, the Board's Chief Chemist, A T Wilford suggested that the Board might return to bus roofs having aluminium paint applied as such treatment resulted in lower temperatures being maintained in the saloons during warmer weather. W A C Snook, in his position as Acting Chief Engineer, agreed to this proposal but he was soon overruled by Durrant who decided that no changes should be made to the current procedure. It was not until the following May that the post war colour scheme was finally agreed which involved the window surround of the upper deck windows being painted cream and the upper deck roof to be the same colour as the remainder of the body in lieu of brown which had been specified earlier.

Although the involvement of RT 46 in the preparatory work for the 3/2RT2/2 conversion appears largely forgotten, the vehicle was soon to take part in another, better-remembered demonstration. In order to determine the arrangement of route number and destination indicators on the 3RT3, a series of tests were conducted in October 1946. Having been withdrawn from service and sent to Chiswick for two months commencing 1 September, RT 46 was on site when a vehicle was needed to demonstrate the existing display. Taking place when most of the Board's buses were operating with restricted blinds, RT 46 received a full set including an example for the rear roof box; the arrangement pitched against a new blind layout using RT 110. The front roofbox from RT 110 had been removed and the canopy panel above the bonnet reduced to replicate that of the prototype. As the front ultimate destination of a 2RT2 was shown above the intermediate points served, a board in reversed style was clipped in place on both buses; flat beading fixed below the front upper deck windows to which fasteners were fitted allowed the boards to overlay tightly the existing blind boxes. The display demonstrated by RT 110 was the wider, the route number being shown to the nearside of the intermediate points (the clips holding it in place remaining in situ long after the bus re-entered service). RT 46 had been equipped with a route number stencil plate holder on the front corner pillar, which was similar but not identical to that fitted to RT 19. This modification required the removal of a handrail at this point, another forming part of the new fitting. Set at 45 degrees, the display was installed on the eighty 2RT2s operating from Putney Bridge garage only; it was later to be included in the specification for the RT3.

The absence of a front roof box from the body of RT 110 made it an ideal candidate for displaying the post-war blind layout. RT 110 appears in a somewhat hybrid livery with white paint applied to the window surrounds of both decks but with a red instead of a grey or brown roof. With the canopy stencil removed, the route number appears to the nearside of the vehicle although the centring of the whole display does not occur until the second example. Later with the stencil plate replaced beneath the canopy, RT 110 parades twice with another 2RT2, presumably RT 46, and STL 706 to determine the ease in identifying the route numbers of buses lined up together at one stop. The corner number applied to the STL was found to weaken the body structure.

The under canopy view of RT 19 shows the position of the hooter, no doubt taped in place for effect, and the corner pillar route number whose design differs from those eventually to be fixed to the 2RT2s operated by Putney Bridge. The bell cord pierces the original under canopy stencil plate position to terminate near an oblong nearside mirror. The pairing of RT 1's body and RT 19's chassis survived a six-week overhaul in the spring of 1951, after which the bus saw out its final days in passenger service at Putney Bridge garage. It was withdrawn on 1 November 1953 and seconded briefly to the training fleet but presumably saw little use, prompting Durrant to seek authority to hand over the chassis to Chiswick Training School and for the body to be destroyed. Nevertheless, it was renumbered 9744 upon removal on 6 April 1954 and retained. It was then mounted on the chassis from SRT 45 to form 1019J (Mobile Training Unit) on 5 October. In this guise, it continued to exist until mounted on the chassis of RT 1420 in June 1956, the resulting vehicle numbered 1037J. This vehicle is now restored as RT 1 and in the safekeeping of the London Bus Preservation Trust.

Also considered at this time was the continuance and possible illumination of the offside rear stencil plate. A document describing the test was produced to which was appended photographs of the vehicles involved although an additional unidentified 2RT2 was used to demonstrate the offside route stencil in position, the vehicle used being painted in original livery adopted for the type. It was not until 1 January 1948 that the recommendations in the report were considered by the newly formed London Transport Executive. With Lord Latham in the chair, those in attendance opted for the display demonstrated by RT 110 but there remained three items for later attention.

1) The offside route number should be central in the panel pressing; on the demonstration bus this was located against the forward edge of the panel.
2) The route number display beneath the canopy should have its opening section painted, presumably in a contrasting colour, in order to provide a frame for the blind.
3) An experimental offside illuminated blind should be prepared as an alternative to the route number plate. This was to be fitted to a vehicle and presented later.

At the same time, the Executive also agreed to discontinue the crown advertising bills placed either side of the front destination; a decision later rescinded.

The agreements with Park Royal and Weymann had been signed in anticipation of the first RT3 bodies being produced during 1946. Such expectations failed to be realised and both companies were compelled to inform the Board that delivery could not be expected until February 1947, their estimated combined output for the year being 511. Once the delay was announced, Durrant ordered a full review of the situation, which confirmed acute shortages of skilled labour and materials had hampered production. The delay resulted in consideration being given to resuming the manufacturing of bodies on an in-house basis for delivery from early 1948. W F Sinclair, Deputy General Manager (Road Services), secured a remit from the Chairman's meeting held on 14 November 1946 by which he was requested to ensure that in-house production started as soon as possible. His report entitled 'Manufacture of Bus Bodies by the Board – Utilisation of Existing Premises' was presented to the Chairman's Meeting held on 27 February 1947.

The cab of RT 19 displays some of the modifications planned for the post-war RT. Unknown hands have contrived to remove the droop of the cab window using either paint or coloured tape to produce the desired effect. The rear view of RT 19 shows it still carrying RT 1's registration number.

The lower deck interior finds the handrail removed from beneath the farechart that has been transferred using a temporary frame to the approved post-war position. A bell cord runs the length of the lower saloon to replace the two bell pushes recessed into the ceiling. The handrails above the three seats and unique to this body remain in place. Note the uneven application of the figure '9' to the rear wall fleet number.

Sinclair prefaced his submission by stating that his line of thinking had centred on a strategy that would complement the current construction programme for new buses. His plan focused upon using Chiswick tram depot as a body building works, where the initial conversion would not be expensive and its close proximity to Chiswick works a distinct advantage. The report also advocated the conversion of Hampstead tram depot to an overhaul facility for the miscellaneous fleet and possibly bus body accident repairs, Chiswick tram depot having been previously identified as the base for both.

Before any action could be taken, Sinclair considered it necessary to consult with the National Union of Vehicle Builders regarding an increase in rates of pay for members of the Chiswick workforce likely to become involved in the construction of new bodies. This he thought essential due to rates of remuneration being higher for those employed by outside companies. However, in order that union negotiations did not hinder the project, Sinclair recommended that plans and estimates be prepared for the conversion of Chiswick and Hampstead tram depots that would allow work to commence immediately once labour difficulties had been settled.

The scheme lingered on for a few weeks following the February report but on 20 March, Sinclair advised those attending the Chairman's meeting that as the rates of pay remained an issue, he was investigating an alternative proposal by which bus bodies could be produced at a swifter rate. His proposal sought to explore the possibility of Park Royal and Weymann producing additional bodies over and above the contracted quantities and not to pursue the Chiswick proposal.

At this time, the Board called for comparisons between the cost of bodies manufactured for the 2RT2 and those ordered for the 3RT3. In response, G F Sinclair produced a detailed analysis in which he gave the cost for producing an early wartime, Chiswick built RT body as £948 rising to £1,232 if an outside manufacturer had undertaken the work. However, this cost had been inflated to include all preparatory work for an anticipated long production run, which, if deducted, would have brought the normal cost of an RT2 body to £850 for an in-house product that equated with £1,100 if bought from elsewhere. The cost for producing an RT3 body was given as £2,000, this being a provisional estimate calculated following consultation with the manufacturers and based upon the current level of wages and price of materials. The specifications for the vehicles were not alike, the RT2 body being designed as a composite wood and metal structure, whereas the RT3 was largely of metal construction. Grounds for the increase were given as the general post-war rise in manufacturing costs and the many technical improvements incorporated.

Writing on 13 February 1947, Sinclair recorded that very few RT bodies had been delivered by Park Royal and Weymann and no complete vehicles had yet been taken into stock. Investigations had been conducted to ensure that a fair share of the companies' total output was being received, the revised agreement requiring Park Royal to allocate 40% and Weymann 35% of their total output to the Board. As in the case of all highly jigged and tooled products, some eighteen months of preparatory work had been necessary at the body builders due to the fabrication of the framework, the method of using materials being at some variance with the processes currently used. In order to meet the Board's requirements, separate shops had now been established at both factories, the contractors giving an assurance that they would be able to meet their future delivery programmes with labour being diverted from other contracts when necessary. As an aside, Sinclair recorded that had the Board accepted the manufacturers' standard products in 1945, it would have an additional 175 buses available although these would not have been entirely suitable. This scenario was never considered, as substantial deliveries of RT bodies were expected from June 1946. In the outcome, the programme ran 13 months behind schedule, Sinclair under-predicting that some 152 RTs would be in stock by the end of the year with 29 bodies per month being produced at Park Royal and 21 at Weymann from the beginning of 1948.

Among the assortment of vehicles in the licensing shop at Chiswick can be seen the two 8ft wide vehicle test rigs, both utilising standard RT3 chassis and both having their wheel tracks widened with special spacer studs placed between the hubs and wheel centres. Slight differences in the body construction of each test vehicle will be noted.

Few photographs exist of the many jigs required in order to construct the RT3 body to exacting tolerances. Two removable panels were installed on the offside of the RT: that to the rear provided access to the battery compartment, that more forward, to the RP lubricator. The jig in use here ensures that the fixing points are correctly aligned.

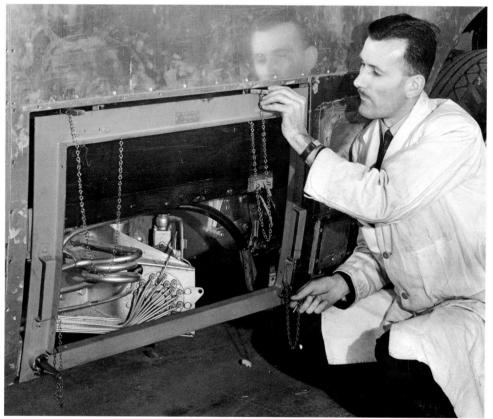

Launching the RT3

Why J H Brebner, the Board's Chief Public Relations Officer, chose Tottenham garage to introduce the RT to members of the press is unrecorded. Nevertheless, on 20 January 1947, he revealed that the first of 500 new post-war buses, which 'were superior to any bus used in public transport would soon appear on the streets'. His statement continues:

(The bus) will be 120hp oil engined double-decker seating 56 passengers. By reason of its many improvements over previous models, it is a vehicle of which London Transport is very proud and of which it is believed Londoners in general will be equally proud. It has luxury expanded rubber seating. Long research and development have been made to obtain the ideal passenger seating position, both from the point of view of riding comfort and ease of getting in and out. Skeleton seats have been constructed with all types of passengers – heavy and light, tall and short. The back of the seat is inclined at an angle of 17 degrees, which combines the maximum rest for the seated passenger with the greatest ease of getting up. The new bus has improved suspension, which gives smoother and better riding. The six-cylinder power unit has improved rubber mounting which eliminates engine vibration and lessens noise. The body is a special all-metal one evolved after long research by the Board's engineers.

The driver of London Transport's new bus has also been carefully studied. From this point of view, the bus may be said to be the last word in development. It is almost effortless to drive. It has a pneumatic pre-selective gear change effected by a small gate gear lever on the steering column. A foot pedal actuates the pneumatic mechanism, which is no heavier in operation than an ordinary accelerator pedal. The powerful brakes also are pneumatic and here too the brake pedal controlling this 12-ton vehicle is just as light as the gear change pedal. This brake pedal incorporates a special safety feature, evolved by the Board's engineers, which gives protection against inadvertent emergency brake application, which might cause discomfort and alarm to the passengers. This is done by the action of an auxiliary spring, which only comes into operation over the last part of pedal travel and thus necessitates a much higher foot pressure to obtain an emergency application.

The driver's cabin is larger than on any existing bus. Its ventilation has been the subject of special research. The windscreen is in two adjustable parts. The frontal window arrangement gives the driver the most complete field of vision on any bus or car. The bus, by its mechanical perfection relieves the driver of fatigue as far as humanly possible – an important contribution to road safety. The bus is lubricated automatically and has been specially designed to require the minimum of maintenance in service.

Although Brebner was relatively accurate in describing the RT body as being of all-metal construction, a significant amount of timber remained within the framework, most noticeably in the cross bars beneath the lower deck floor, their design differing little from the timber beam strengthened by the insertion of a metal flitch plate used to support the RT2 body. The vertical pillars dividing each bay were constructed from mild steel channel loaded with timber; this revised composite form of construction provided easier fixing and removal of both interior and exterior panels during overhaul or in the event

RT 559 was taken in to LT stock at the beginning of June 1948 and here shows the classic lines of a new 3RT3 recently outshopped from Weymann's factory in Addlestone, Surrey.

of damage. In each bay, horizontal girders with weight reduction/strengthening holes similar to those used in the construction of the RT2 body, continued to provide lateral strength, give support for the lower deck windows and act as an anchorage point for the top of the seat frames. A girder of lighter construction was used for the same purpose in the framework of the upper deck. Much of the timber used in the body and in the cab construction was of intricate design, which meant keeping some shaping machines at the overhaul works in order to mass-produce replacements.

The double-skinned roof of the RT2 was improved for the RT3, by using a single aluminium sheet for the upper surface and a single panel produced by Jicwood Ltd for the ceiling; the cavity between the panels contained an insulation material. Jicwood Ltd was a subsidiary of the Airscrew Company of Weybridge and although the design was considered an important development, an experiment involving six RTs later explored the best methods of repair.

Notwithstanding the methods employed in constructing the framework for the RT3 bodies, the outward design remained greatly influenced by the RT2 body produced at Chiswick. Of course there were many differences, some subtle, others obvious such as the transfer of the fare chart from the platform to the offside rear of the lower saloon where a bell cord replaced the two bell pushes recessed into the ceiling. The interior colour scheme of cream, green and brown Rexines remained, although the vertical window shrouds were much shorter requiring bridging sections above and below each fixed and opening light. The seat frames used a better grade of alloy, the steel tubular sections being painted brown instead of green, while a new style of seat moquette was introduced using the same colours as used for the RT2 but woven into a different pattern. The horizontal handrail below the farechart on the RT2 was discontinued; its replacement – a vertical grab rail to the offside of the lower saloon entrance – became a later modification.

RT3 bodies produced by Park Royal and Weymann were virtually identical apart, of course, from the bonnet and body number series allocated and the body builder's plate. Yet the more keen-eyed would have noticed a slight difference in length of the half-round beading that terminated adjacent to the offside bottom corner of the front windscreen, that on Weymann bodies being fractionally shorter. Another clue could be found under each seat cushion where the seat frame locating blocks were stamped with the initials of the manufacturing companies: PRV for Park Royal Vehicles and W for Weymann. Soon after the post-war RT's introduction, a bus inspector suggested the body builder's plate be shifted from the platform to an area inside the lower saloon. His idea was prompted by young bus enthusiasts jumping on to the platform of the brand new buses to ascertain the make of the body. This suggestion was rejected.

On 10 May 1947, RT 402 with Weymann body entered service from Leyton garage having been licensed the previous day, followed by RT 152 with Park Royal body on 23 May. After a false start, the RT was now in full production.

When RT 402 entered service, restricted blind layouts were set to last a further three years and in consequence, body manufacturers were required to apply paint to some areas of glass fronting the blind box apertures. As London began an extensive programme of reconstruction, the new 3RT3s helped provide some optimism for a brave post war world.

In its recently-delivered condition, RT 152 conforms with an earlier directive that called for the deletion of the offside route number stencil; a decision subsequently rescinded. Also of note is the black unpainted rubber moulding used to glaze the window pans, that on the 2RT2 being painted white. No water chutes from the top deck formed part of the initial specification for the RT.

RT 154 was delivered new to Croydon garage in early July 1947 and is seen here some five years later operating from the former 2RT2 stronghold at Putney Bridge. Having been subjected to two overhauls, the bus is now finished in the all-red livery adopted by the Board in 1950. It still carries a small offside route number of a type installed much earlier as an interim measure.

Holloway garage took delivery
of RT 744 on 16 June 1948,
its Park Royal body being
equipped with an offside
route number stencil holder
and smaller headlamps when
compared with those fitted
to the earliest post-war RTs.
All variations in design were
approved at meetings of
the Board's Main Technical
Committee.

Some passengers aboard the first Park Royal-bodied RT into service are no doubt eagerly awaiting a journey on London Transport's latest bus. The first vehicles delivered were equipped with sprung-case seat cushions and their effect on riding qualities of the vehicle can only be imagined. The platform is edged with Adamite, a non-slip covering that was eventually replaced with the more-traditional pyramid tread plate. The white disc introduced during the early months of the war 'for the benefit of trolleybus drivers' was quickly removed from all the Board's buses in April 1948 after a visit by members of the British Transport Commission to Chiswick works. The inward sweep of the lowest offside corner panel remained unique to the 2RT2, the design of the 3RT3 calling for a panel with a single curve.

RT 97 and RTC 1

Few members of the 2RT2 fleet suffered during the London Blitz as most were laid up during the aerial onslaught that wreaked havoc on the capital from September 1940 until May 1941. Nevertheless, during this time, RTs 16 and RT 99 underwent minor bodywork repairs due to damage resulting from enemy action. The V1 campaign against the capital that began in April 1944, however, did seriously damage four members of the class in circumstances described in the Board's daily record of events.

The first incident occurred at 10.15am on 18 June 1944 when a V1 (initially designated 'pilotless aircraft') exploded in Upper Richmond Road, Putney. RT 87 running on route 37 from Chelverton Road garage as AF4 was blown over. The bus crew, Driver Slatter and Conductor Wright, were treated in hospital for cuts and four passengers were injured; two later died. As previously recorded, the bus was sent to Chiswick where it received the recently overhauled body from RT 52. The bus returned to passenger service on 1 July, its original body eventually being repaired and fitted to RT 66. On 27 June 1944 at 12.40pm a V1 exploded at the junction of Highbury Corner and Upper Street. RT 59 running as AF8 on route 30 was wrecked but ST 413 (running as J18 on route 4A) and STL 1784 (running as B25 on route 19) lost only their windows. A number of persons were taken to hospital including Driver Marshall from Chelverton Road garage who suffered shock. RT 59 was sent to Birmingham Corporation for repair; on its return, the absence of the canopy extension below the central band showed that a non-standard reconstruction had occurred; the bus re-entered revenue service 1 January 1945. Perhaps the most harrowing of all the 2RT2 V1 incidents was the one at 12.14pm on 30 June 1944 at the junction of Howland Street and Tottenham Court Road where the body of RT 66 was blown to pieces. Driver Perry and Conductress Watling were killed. What remained of the body from RT 66 was not separated from its chassis until 20 July 1944; on 26 August Chiswick fitted the repaired body from RT 87. RT 66 re-entered service at Putney Bridge on 29 September. The final V1 explosion involving a 2RT2 occurred at 5.55pm on 27 July 1944 at Gainsborough Road in Hackney, ten yards from the terminus of route 30. Eight buses were involved – six from Hackney garage and two 2RT2s from Chelverton Road – all described as blasted. No injuries were reported although an inspector suffered shock. The 2RT2 most seriously damaged was RT 97 running as AF20; it was later towed to Chiswick. From surviving documents, it would appear that the LTPB maintained a special relationship with Liverpool Corporation and Birmingham City transport departments. Visits by members of Durrant's team were made to both undertakings to compare working practices. The Board turned to Birmingham to repair RTs 59 and 97; both buses were dispatched to Tyburn Road works, Erdington, on 26 August 1944.

The reason for Tyburn Road being incapable of undertaking repairs to RT 97 remains undocumented but it produced a dramatic change in destiny for the bus that began following its return on 14 December 1944 to Chiswick. The bus was selected, with two STLs and two trolleybuses, for adaptation to a Pay As You Board configuration, all five vehicles differing in layout although each employed a seated conductor. The decision to undertake such alteration during wartime conditions is questionable; however, fare collection had become a major topic of discussions between the Post War Planning Committee and the Board's senior officers during 1942/43 and the PAYB tests were undoubtedly an extension of the many proposals put forward.

RT 97's V1 bomb-damaged body was rebuilt for PAYB operation by increasing the size of the rear platform to produce a large circulating area. A conductor's desk was installed over the nearside wheel arch, producing a loss of 6 lower deck seats. The vehicle was fitted with electro-pneumatically operated sliding platform doors, some innovation being necessary to maintain the required 3ft minimum entrance width. The design team overcame this problem by using two sliding doors, each half the width of the opening and arranged to run on parallel tracks with a result that the inner door enclosed the forward half of the doorway and the outer door completed the operation. To allow the two doors to travel sufficiently far forward, the corner pillar was removed and set some 6in inside the bus, thereby removing the nearside route stencil panel. This allowed the doors, which were mounted on the outside, to advance as far as the rear wheel arch resulting in a clear entrance 3ft 4in wide. The Board patented the design of the doors and entrusted the manufacture of the operating equipment to G D Peters & Co. At the time of writing Peters Door Systems Ltd of Braintree, Essex, continues to manufacture sliding door systems for trains and buses. The conductor controlled the doors by pressing a foot-operated push button, to pass compressed air to either end of the door engine resulting in alternate opening and closing movements. This engine was mounted behind two inspection flaps hinged on the outside of the bus, both located within and above the central dividing band. RT 97 had been overhauled and converted to 1/2RT2/1 configuration three months before the Gainsborough Road incident and it was from its revised system that compressed air was drawn for door operation, the storage tank holding enough air for six door operations after the engine had been stopped. In case of emergency two air discharge valves were provided and upon their release, the doors could be worked by hand. Due to the fitting of doors and their mechanism, some structural alterations to the bus framework became necessary and a strong, deep metal girder was installed from the resited corner pillar to that on the rear nearside. Now that the platform was completely enclosed, an emergency door was built on the offside of the platform directly opposite the sliding doors. Other emergency exits were in the rear upper deck window as in normal practice and the lower deck rear platform framing, both having identical means of opening.

Over a year was to elapse before the flying bomb damaged RT 97 returned to the streets as part of the pay as you enter experiments. Allocated to Kingston Garage in January 1946 for trials on Route 65, the body had been mainly rebuilt to general 2RT2 configuration but with a revised seating layout on both decks that allowed a seated conductor to collect fares as passengers boarded. As sliding doors were fitted that encased the rear platform, regulations required an additional exit to be installed on the offside of the vehicle.

Little structural change was made to the vehicle after it had been painted green save for the installation of a sliding window behind the conductor's position shown in the photo below. The vehicle operated on route 721 but neither this trial nor the one on route 65 was deemed successful.

The rear platform was completely re-designed and could accommodate 19 standing passengers waiting to pay their fares. To give this expanse of space, the normal staircase was replaced by one of special design positioned over the offside wheel arch. The bottom step continued from the riser giving access to the lower saloon after which a 90-degree turn was necessary to ascend the straight staircase. Due to its position being further forward than usual, on the upper deck it was possible to provide a full width rear seat for four persons. In order to avoid steps within the bus, the rear platform was built to within three inches of the lower deck gangway to which it was connected by a gentle ramp rising between the two wheel arches; as a result, an additional step was required at the entrance. Adequate headroom was maintained on the platform by recessing light bulbs and a transverse handrail into the roof.

Positioned above the rear wheel arch, the conductor faced the foot of the stairs and so had a clear view of all the platform and the lower saloon. All passengers had to pass the pay desk before entering the lower saloon or proceeding upstairs. The sliding doors were offset sufficiently to enable the conductor to see past them to the outside rear of the bus and along the platform edge – a small window had been angled into the bodywork for this purpose. The pay desk swept round the conductor's sitting position, being aligned with the central gangway, achieving maximum width here by the staircase design. The desk was equipped with a ticket-issuing machine provided by the National Cash Register Co and a lockable cash drawer. In addition to the foot-operated switch for operating the doors, the desk had a press button so positioned for the conductor to operate the doors from the platform. A further press button connected to a single acting bell in the driver's cab for communication purposes and to which passengers had no access. To stop the bus, it was necessary to operate either of the two bell pushes in the ceiling of the lower deck, or those in the rear platform wall or at the top of the stairs; all four operated a buzzer so that the driver knew the source of the signal. The driver was also provided with an indicator that illuminated when the doors were open.

The National Cash Register Company provided the ticket issuing equipment installed on RT 97c, seen here after the bus had been painted into Green Line livery for its trials on route 721 from Romford Garage. Although RT 97c was seen as a significant improvement when compared with riding qualities of the Daimler CWA6s then allocated to Romford, its slow loading failed to win support.

Forward of the conductor's position, there were transverse seats for 20 passengers, the bus having the unusual distinction of being one of only a few London double-deck buses in which all passengers sat facing forwards. RT 97 was trimmed in the moquette introduced with the 2RT2 in 1939 and had the same interior colour scheme with Rexine covered cappings around the windows, the material also covering the non-standard mouldings around the staircase and elsewhere. The conversion project was the responsibility of Eric Ottaway whose name appears on the vehicle's record card, which also shows on 31 December 1945 the vehicle achieved an unladen weight of 7t 1cwt. The PAYB buses did not operate simultaneously. The first to enter service was STL 1793 on 25 October 1944. RT 97 entered service on 2 January 1946 from Kingston garage on route 65, where it ran until 25 March 1946. It then ran from Romford between 22 May and 2 July.

RT 97 was first painted in the livery introduced for 2RT2s in 1939, the broken white surround of the lower deck windows being extended to the rear to encompass the windows in the sliding and offside emergency doors. A minor alteration was made before the bus transferred to Romford garage, which involved fitting a sliding window behind the conductor's position. The bus was repainted on 18 April 1946 into the new Green Line livery then only seen on the single-deck coaches. A final embellishment comprised front wheel trims of the type fitted to the 10T10, the only other 2RT2s to have them being RTs 4 and 39 when they appeared in the Victory Parade held in London on 8 June 1946.

The PAYB method of fare collection was deemed unsuccessful and after the trials conducted at Romford garage, RT 97 was returned to Chiswick where it was withdrawn on 6 January 1947. However, the vehicle's future had been assured by the issue, in November 1946 by the Main Technical Committee, of experiment S6248 under the title 'Modifications to RT 97'. Little remains on file of the changes that would be made to RT 97 after withdrawal, the Main Technical Committee receiving no information until 20 July 1948 when a minute headed 'New RTC Double Deck Bus' appeared. The detail it contains is scant.

RT 66 was assigned to the RTC project for testing new aircraft type seating. Two transverse seats were fitted in the lower saloon of RT 66, both having a device fitted that simultaneously altered the angle of seat back and seat cushion; the various settings were recorded on an indicator. There was never any intention of installing passenger-adjustable seats to the RTC, the main object of the experiment (S6248) being to determine whether a fixed seat back angle could give a high standard of comfort to all sizes of passengers; 25 men and 25 women employed at Chiswick works were selected to undertake seat testing. This showed it was possible for a fixed setting to give a large degree of comfort. A forward footrest initially fitted at 1ft 6in was also removed due to the adverse comments received.

On 21 August 1947, details of experiment S6354 were issued to cover the conversion of the chassis from RT 97 to standard 3RT configuration during the 6-month rebuilding programme, which began on 9 June 1948. A 27 May 1948 memorandum requested the fitting of high deflection springs, the PAYB adapted body having been dismounted and the chassis by then resident in the Experimental Shop. Simultaneously, authority was sought to use some of the displaced air pressure equipment from 3RT chassis O961964 (RT 902) to which had been installed a Lockheed servo hydraulic braking system under experiment S6147. The toroidal engine provided for the RTC differed slightly from the A185A. As the existing cylinder block did not allow for the adoption of a standard 3RT (A204) cylinder head, the engine was designated A185B. Careful thought had been given to the provision of adequate heating and ventilation, with the main radiator replaced by two small radiators connected in series and installed beneath the staircase to serve both engine cooling and vehicle heating requirements. The absence of a traditionally placed radiator made possible a new design of driver's cab, whose forward treatment was regarded as an alternative to a full front design and so maintained the high standard of driving visibility synonymous with the 2RT2.

When RTC 1 finally emerged in January 1949, it was described as the Prototype Double Deck Coach. Opportunity was taken during conversion to incorporate features of advanced experimental construction for testing in service. The Development Section at Chiswick soon recognised the high expense of producing RTC 1. As a result, a closer estimate was pursued to assess the economic value of the project. Although still recognisable as an RT, the vehicle had been the subject of a significant makeover. The installation of long windows was achieved by extending the glazed area to the body pillars, now replaced and incorporating additional metalwork to provide a guide for the full drop mechanism installed for each window so equipped. Although opening was limited, the new window abolished the central bar that had become the source of objection in the design of the normal half-drop window.

The Chiswick team meticulously recorded the conversion work to transform RT 97 into the RTC body, some of the most significant being:

Area	Item
Structure	Remove side blind box and destination gear
	Modify inter roof (between decks) to include ventilator scheme
	Fabricate cab and frontal extension
	Undertake upper deck roof widening to include rear ventilator
	Provide pillar replacements with additional metalwork
	Remove conductor's seat and paydesk equipment
	Install conductor's seat and panel work
Cab	Replace screen, side window and quarter light
Seats	Remove 50 seats at 31lb each
	Install 46 seats at 36.25lb each
Windows	Replace drop lights and pans
	Replace fixed lights and pans

At Chiswick on 19 February 1949, the coach achieved an unladen weight of 8 tons, an increase of 19cwt above the weight of RT 97 after conversion for the PAYB tests. The vehicle was initially classified 9RT10 but later 5RT5.

The double leaf sliding doors fitted for the PAYB tests were retained on RTC 1. They operated as follows: to open, both doors moved towards the front of the coach until the inner door was at its fully open position, then the outer door continued to move forwards until fully open. This action was reversed for the doors to close.

Design consultants Norbert Dutton and Douglas Scott had been engaged to assist development of the vehicle's styling, colour schemes and upholstery; the seats were trimmed with loose covers using a new design of moquette. Dark green Rexine was applied to the side walls and the window shrouds were stove-enamelled in a light green although the pillar cappings were finished using polished aluminium covers. The ceiling was painted cream and mottled green linoleum affixed to the floor and areas particularly vulnerable to shoe contact. The familiar flywheel cowl was replaced by a ramp, which extended the width of the body, access provided by means of a removable trap. Much use was made of fluorescent lighting, warm white tubes being installed in both saloons.

The heating and cooling of the saloons was achieved in conjunction with the engine cooling system. During cold weather, air was drawn through the inter-roof space and blown across the radiators into the saloons via ducts on either side. The changeover from heating to cooling was controlled by a single lever positioned beneath the staircase which operated dampers situated in the ducting. In warm weather, air was drawn from the saloons and blown straight to atmosphere via the radiators mounted below the stairs. A pressure release to atmosphere was achieved using a ventilator positioned where once the rear roof box had been sited, the upper deck roof having been modified accordingly.

Trials with the vehicle and subsequent service operation found that there was ample heat available for the two saloons but unfortunately, during relatively warm weather, when little heat was required, the temperature control was insufficient. As a result, passengers were requested to open the windows but during high winds, conditions became uncomfortable due to draughts. A recommendation contained in a subsequent report sought further development of the vehicle's temperature control to allow greater ventilation.

In the month of its completion, the RTC was presented to the press by a demonstration run in late January between Chiswick and Ruislip; one correspondent described it as having a mouth organ front grill. Modifications to the vehicle continued for a further few weeks.

RTC 1 meets the media, members of which demonstrate some of the equipment of the day used for recording still and moving pictures. Behind the small offside rear door could be found the radiators and batteries, this being the only RT2 body (albeit much modified) that provided outside access to the battery compartment. The site formerly occupied by the rear roof box is now a ventilator for the air conditioning system.

Ashtrays affixed to the rear of the seats on the lower deck of RTC 1 confirm that smoking was controversially permitted throughout the coach. Also of note is the absence of a traditional flywheel cover, its place taken by an inclined panel across the width of the bus. The effect of having loose fitted seat covers is obvious.

Norbert Dutton and Douglas Scott were responsible for the interior design of the RTC, the dark green Rexine applied to the sidewalls and window shrouds differing little in shade from that already selected for the RT. A mirror was originally fitted to RT2 bodies at a point on the side of the staircase that would allow the conductor a view of the platform from the rear of the upper deck. Following an experiment to determine the best position, all 2RT2s were equipped with a larger mirror above the staircase for which a wooden bracket was required; a similar mirror was fitted to the RTC. Provision to improve the conductor's view of the upper deck from the platform was included in the specification for the RT3 body, which required the mirror to be recessed into the offside rear ceiling panel.

No luggage space was provided beneath the staircase, the space being occupied by plant for the air conditioning system. Passengers were encouraged to store luggage beneath the seats but this produced a number of negative comments in the final evaluation of the vehicle.

The futuristic look of RTC 1 contrasts dramatically with older vehicles waiting at the traffic lights at Hyde Park Corner.

Once complete, RTC 1 underwent a series of tests under experiment S6387 that considered the repositioning of the engine radiator and the heating and ventilating system. Test 1 took place on 16 March 1949 on an out of service run over route 705, the vehicle initially travelling from Chiswick to Brentford where it followed a coach to Windsor. The new vehicle then ran the whole length of the route to Sevenoaks, returning to Chiswick after completing 108 miles. Minor problems were encountered and, although the riding conditions were reported good, the engine was found somewhat sluggish. Test 2, the following day, took the vehicle over route 711 High Wycombe to Reigate (104 miles covered) and the final out of service test took place on 18 March over route 702 Sunningdale to Gravesend (96 miles). With few problems emerging from the new system, the coach entered passenger service on route 704 on 6 April from Windsor garage having transferred there from Chiswick on 31 March; the overheating problems began almost immediately. Over the next two weeks, the bus occasionally returned to Chiswick having operated only on 6-9 and 15-17 April. During the second session, average loadings were noted before 10am but during the following twelve hours the coach became fully laden with standing passengers on some journeys. On 18 April, the RTC was to have transferred to Hertford garage but was received at Chiswick following a report that a water loss had occurred overnight. With a recalcitrant valve replaced, the coach did move to Hertford garage where it entered service from 20 April on route 715 Hertford to Guildford. Until 2 May, the coach ran half-full for the early part of the day and with a full passenger complement from mid-day to early evening; only one instance of overheating was reported. From early May, RTC 1 was allocated to Reigate and later to Hemel Hempstead, Windsor and Hertford garages. It was then demoted to bus work, its Green Line duties having concluded after just nine months.

Door control was provided by G D Peters, the doors the company provided for RT 97 being reused on the RTC.

The engine fitted to RTC 1 is described as A185B, the vehicle's log card carrying the warning: 2RT engine converted to 3RT not interchangeable with 3RT.

The first criticisms about the design of the coach appeared in July 1949 and could be summed up under three headings. The first took exception to the type of seating employed that permitted a capacity of only 46, operating economics suggesting that if a double-deck vehicle were adopted for Green Line operation, a capacity of more than 50 should be the aim. Second, the under-seat provision for luggage was not satisfactory, passengers decrying the absence of an overhead rack in order to deposit hats, coats and other small personal items. Finally, the slight swaying motion when travelling at speed and pitching when accelerating were disliked. Also criticised but dealt with separately was the decision to allow smoking on both decks. The immediate response to the seating issue was a suggestion for the installation of a less luxurious type which according to B H Harbour, Operating Manager Country Buses and Coaches, could be increased on the RTC to 55 if standard seating were installed or 54 should a customised RT be adopted for use on Green Line routes. Modifications to the stabilising equipment and front suspension would address the issue of movement but no immediate response to the lack of luggage space could be found other than to utilise the space beneath the staircase.

Another area attracting adverse comment arose from capital costs. An estimate of £5,000 per vehicle was based on a bulk order for 150 RTC vehicles each equipped with 55 seats, giving an average cost per seated passenger of £91. The current price of £3,250 for a modern 35-seat single-deck coach and £4,550–£4,700 (depending on the number ordered) for a 54-seat RT, equipped with doors and heating, provided an average cost per seated passenger of £93 and £84–£87 respectively. With coaches being used on journeys of approximately one-hour's duration and knowing the obvious qualities of the standard RT, the purchase of further coaches based on the RTC became difficult to justify. In stating that the public might eventually be won over in accepting double-deck coaches on Green Line routes, Harbour kept his opinion that the performance of such vehicles had not yet reached a point that justified their eventual wholesale adoption. However, he recognised that double-deck Daimlers had been used continuously on routes 721 and 722 since their reintroduction in 1946. Yet these routes were considered untypical of Green Line services by operating through the densely populated East End where an excess of short journey passengers was carried.

The log card for RTC 1 incorrectly states that the vehicle was demoted to bus work on 30 December 1949, the former coach actually entering service from Leatherhead garage on 23 December after modifications at Chiswick. Under this programme, the saloon heating system became redundant and its control damper was fixed to prevent air from passing directly into the saloon. Further changes facilitated an increased airflow over the radiator, a different design having replaced the original arrangement. In this condition, the RTC was tested on route 705 on 21 December when engine temperatures were found to be substantially lower than those experienced earlier in the year.

The remainder of the RTC story is one of decline, although its initial existence served to demonstrate that especially produced double-deck vehicles for Green Line coach duties were not required.

Had things turned out differently, FXT 272 would not have been the only 2RT chassis to receive a newer body. Following completion of the 3/2RT conversion programme, it soon became apparent to Durrant's team that the Board was now in possession of a number of chassis whose life had been significantly extended by modification. During 1952, a member of the team suggested that bodies from the SRT class could be transferred to 3/2RT chassis. A further report received in November 1952 placed an approximate cost of £35,000 on the scheme but envisaged some problems that related to body mounting and standardisation as a likely cause for some resistance. No further action was taken and the RT bodies mounted on adapted STL chassis, to produce the SRT class, were later fitted to new 3RT chassis.